The Buildings of
London Zoo

ROYAL
COMMISSION
ON THE HISTORICAL
MONUMENTS
OF ENGLAND

The Buildings of

London Zoo

Peter Guillery

ROYAL COMMISSION ON THE HISTORICAL MONUMENTS OF ENGLAND

Published by the Royal Commission on the Historical Monuments of England,
Fortress House, 23 Savile Row, London W1X 2JQ

First published 1993

ISBN 1 873592 15 9

British Library Cataloguing in Publication Data
A CIP catalogue record for this book is available from the British Library

Designed by Chuck Goodwin, 27 Artesian Road, London W2 5DA

Printed by BAS Printers Ltd, Over Wallop, Stockbridge, Hampshire SO20 8JD

Contents

Illustrations

Commissioners

Chairman's Foreword

London Zoo became a focus of public attention in 1991 when the Zoological Society of London announced that its financial position necessitated the closure of its Regent's Park establishment. Most of the public concern was centred on the future of the animals, but a question mark also arose over the future of the buildings. London Zoo is a singular architectural complex: 'Noah's Ark and the Tower of Babel combined', in the words of Ian Nairn. The Zoo has a number of outstanding and unusual buildings that are exhibits in their own right. Taken as a whole the buildings of the Zoo can tell us much about the history of animal display over a period spanning nearly 170 years, as well as inform the broader concerns of architectural history, particularly the process of design and construction.

For these reasons the Royal Commission on the Historical Monuments of England (RCHME) decided to undertake a comprehensive but rapid survey of the buildings of London Zoo as part of its continuing national programme of emergency recording of buildings threatened with demolition or alteration. The field-work was carried out in early 1992; since then the threat of closure has waxed and waned. At the time of writing the future of London Zoo remains uncertain. Whatever transpires it is probable that the site and its buildings will undergo significant changes.

The survey that forms the basis of this book presents a portrait of London Zoo as it was in 1992. Every structure was recorded by at least one photograph and by field notes. The primary record, more extensive than is published here, comprises photographs, notes and supplementary information from published and unpublished sources. It is held by the RCHME's National Monuments Record at Fortress House, 23 Savile Row, London W1X 2JQ.

Relatively few of London Zoo's buildings are statutorily listed as being of special architectural or historic interest, although the whole Zoo is within a Conservation Area. The Royal Commission's purpose differs from that of the listing programme so the architectural and historic importance recognised herein does not necessarily satisfy the criteria required for statutory protection.

This publication is intended to inform a broad range of interests. London Zoo holds fascination, and evokes memories, for a great many people. Certain buildings are well known, but they have not previously been examined in the context of a general survey of the Zoo. Building and rebuilding has taken place almost continuously at London Zoo since 1827. Fortunately, representative examples of virtually every phase of Zoo architecture survive. The buildings are as varied and exotic as the animals. They are, to quote Ian Nairn again, 'a good match for nature's craziness'.

The Commissioners would like to thank all the staff involved in this project, especially Peter Guillery, Derek Kendall and Andrew Donald, for the speed and quality of their work. Commissioners also wish to thank David Jones who, as the Director of London Zoo, agreed to our survey, and the staff of the Zoo for providing access to the buildings.

PARK OF MONMOUTH

Acknowledgements

The investigation of the buildings, the documentary research and the writing of the text were carried out by Peter Guillery and the plans were prepared by Andrew Donald in the course of their work for the Royal Commission's London Threatened Buildings Section. The photographs were taken by Derek Kendall and printed by James Davies, Peter Murphy and Mike Seaforth. The project was encouraged and supported by John Bold and Robin Thornes. Other Royal Commission staff who gave valuable help were Charlotte Bradbeer, Stephen Croad, Samantha Kelly, Diane Kendall, Ian Leith and Joanna Smith. The Commissioners who provided advice were Bridget Cherry, Kerry Downes, Gwyn Meirion-Jones, Anne Riches and Charles Thomas. Editing, design and production were managed by Kate Owen; Jan Cornell prepared the manuscript for typesetting, and Chuck Goodwin designed the book.

The Royal Commission gratefully acknowledges the co-operation of the Zoological Society of London and Zoo Operations Limited, and in particular help from Peter Denton, Reginald Fish, Peter Humphreys, Dot Price, Graham Roden and Colin Wears. Others who have assisted with the preparation of this book include: Ove Arup and Partners; John S Bonnington and Partners; the Casson Conder Partnership; Roger Cline; Emap Architecture; English Heritage (London Region), particularly Susie Barson; Gary Gabriel Associates; R W Guillery; the Institution of Civil Engineers Library; the Royal Institute of British Architects, British Architectural Library and Drawings Collection; John Toovey; Malcolm Tucker; the Twentieth Century Society; the Victorian Society; and the City of Westminster, Marylebone Local History Library.

All the photographs, figures and plans are RCHME copyright unless otherwise stated. The following organisations kindly allowed reproduction of their material: Aerofilms Limited (Fig 12); Alti-Cam/David M Kay (Fig 77); the Casson Conder Partnership (Figs 38 and 41); Emap Architecture (Fig 41); and the Zoological Society of London (Frontispiece to Chapter 1, Figs 4, 8, 14, 15, 17, 18, 22, 23, 27, 28, 68 and 103, and the base plan used for Plan 4).

Editorial Notes

The Buildings of London Zoo begins with a chapter on the historical development of the Zoo site and its buildings between 1826 and 1992. Subsequent chapters consist of a gazetteer of the surviving structures, each chapter dealing with a particular building type (for example, Animal Houses, Aviaries).

Within each chapter, the buildings and structures are described in chronological order by type. The name given for each building or structure is the name in use in 1992; any previous names or uses are explained in the gazetteer text (for example, the Parrot House was originally designed and built as the Refreshment Rooms). All the buildings of substance have a reference number (for example, Plan 4:33) that allows it to be located on Plan 4 (1991), which is printed at the back of the book for ease of reference, along with Plans 1 to 3, for comparative purposes.

In most cases the main facts of the building history are summarised in the margin, in italics, to give at a glance the key dates and the names of the architects and others involved, with some other pertinent information. Specific sources are listed at the end of each entry and general sources at the end of the book.

Anyone who wishes to gain access to the original survey field notes, photographs and other archive materials should refer to the List of Recorded Buildings at the end of the book, where reference is made to the National Buildings Record File Numbers.

Unless otherwise stated, all the photographs in this book were taken in the period December 1991 to July 1992. Picture sources are given at the end of each caption. For pictures held by the Royal Commission, the following codes have been used:

BB	National Buildings Record photographic coverage London Zoo
NMR/APU	Air Photography Unit photographic reference
RCHME	Miscellaneous/archive collections

For pictures held by other bodies, the following codes have been used:

BAL, RIBA Drawings Collection	British Architectural Library, Royal Institute of British Architects Drawings Collection (Heinz Gallery)
ZSL	Zoological Society of London

1
Historical
Development

The Camel House (now the Clock Tower) (from a lithograph by F W Hulme).

1826 to 1900

The Zoological Society of London was formed in 1826. Sir Stamford Raffles (1781–1826) was its founder and first President and support was given by Sir Humphry Davy, President of the Royal Society. This was the world's first institution devoted to the study and display of animals. In so far as there was a model, it was the Jardin des Plantes in Paris, which included a menagerie. The Society was given land in Regent's Park by the Crown to accommodate a collection of animals and Decimus Burton (1800–81) was commissioned to lay out gardens around pens and cages. Burton had established himself as an architect through working with John Nash, a friend of his father. He had already seen his designs executed in the Royal Parks, his work including some of the Regent's Park terraces. Burton's plans for the Zoological Gardens were complete in 1827 and the first 5 acres (2 ha) were laid out and opened in April 1828. Admission was restricted to members of the Society or their guests until 1846 when the general public was admitted.

The gardens initially comprised a small triangle on the south side of the road that is now the Outer Circle, an informal enclave with meandering paths and a raised terrace [1 and 2]. Light ornamental buildings were scattered in a manner comparable to the arrangement of earlier menageries in private gardens. From the outset the Society had at its disposal a 6-acre (2·4 ha) strip north of the Outer Circle and south of the Regent's Canal (the area now known as the Middle Gardens). This was not developed until 1829–30, the expansion following the granting of a Royal Charter

1 London Zoo in 1829 (from The Zoological Keepsake, 1830, as reproduced in H Scherren The Zoological Society of London, *1905).*

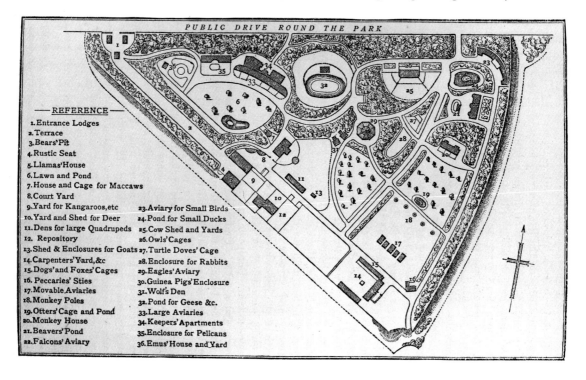

PUBLIC DRIVE ROUND THE PARK

—— REFERENCE ——
1. Entrance Lodges
2. Terrace
3. Bears' Pit
4. Rustic Seat
5. Llamas' House
6. Lawn and Pond
7. House and Cage for Maccaws
8. Court Yard
9. Yard for Kangaroos, etc
10. Yard and Shed for Deer
11. Dens for large Quadrupeds
12. Repository
13. Shed & Enclosures for Goats
14. Carpenters' Yard, &c
15. Dogs' and Foxes' Cages
16. Peccaries' Sties
17. Movable Aviaries
18. Monkey Poles
19. Otters' Cage and Pond
20. Monkey House
21. Beavers' Pond
22. Falcons' Aviary
23. Aviary for Small Birds
24. Pond for Small Ducks
25. Cow Shed and Yards
26. Owls' Cages
27. Turtle Doves' Cage
28. Enclosure for Rabbits
29. Eagles' Aviary
30. Guinea Pigs' Enclosure
31. Wolf's Den
32. Pond for Geese &c.
33. Large Aviaries
34. Keepers' Apartments
35. Enclosure for Pelicans
36. Emus' House and Yard

in 1829. A tunnel, the present East Tunnel [93], was built under the road to link the two precincts and the land was laid out. A semicircular carriage sweep, opposite the entrance lodges, and a terrace walk, along the top of the canal's south bank, are original features that substantially survive [Plan 2]. In 1831 the main triangle was enlarged to 10 acres (4 ha), the Middle Gardens were enlarged by 1 acre (0·4 ha) and 3 acres (1·2 ha) were taken on the north side of the canal. There was further expansion to the south in 1834 with the addition of 10 more acres (4 ha), giving a total area for the gardens of 30 acres (12 ha). The land north of the canal was given up in 1841 in exchange for a westwards expansion of the Middle Gardens.

Burton was formally appointed Architect to the Society in 1830, a post he retained until 1841. His early animal buildings have been neatly described as 'follies set in an elegant garden for entertainment and curiosity'.[1] Of these nothing survives, though the Clock Tower [13, 14 and 15] and the Raven's Cage [72 and 73] are rebuildings of 1820s structures that give an indication of the initial scale and approach. They endure not as animal accommodation but simply as decorative objects commemorating the early gardens. Three Island Pond [Plan 4:57] is a surviving landscape feature from the early gardens and the East Tunnel's classical south portal is a reminder that Burton was working in the context of John Nash's Regent's Park.

2 London Zoo from the north in 1829 (from The Zoological Keepsake, *1830, as reproduced in H Scherren* The Zoological Society of London, *1905).*

Decimus Burton's buildings

3 The Elephant Stables in 1835; Decimus Burton, architect (from C F Partington, National History and Views of London, *1835, drawn by T H Shepherd, engraved by J Shury).*

Amongst Burton's animal houses of 1830–1 were thatched 'elephant stables', in a style which blended the gothick and the classical [**3**], and a 'Tuscan' Brahmin Bull House [**4**]. The picturesque *cottage orné* character of these buildings reflected current practice in ornamental garden architecture. Given the aura of novelty that surrounded the zoological gardens it is, perhaps, surprising that the buildings were not more exotic. This is exhibition architecture; little thought appears to have been given to the peculiar requirements of animal housing and display.

4 The Brahmin Bull House in 1831; Decimus Burton, architect (from a lithograph by J Hakewill).

Burton's later zoo architecture is represented by the Giraffe House of 1836–7, which survives although much rebuilt [**16**]. This modest classical shed, tall to meet its purpose, eschews showiness with an approach that seems rooted more in the functionalism that characterised contemporary industrial architecture than in ornamental garden architecture.

By 1850 the gardens had expanded eastwards and southwards almost to their current boundaries. They were a popular success and other zoos had, by then, opened across the world. The name 'zoo' was popularised in 1867 by 'The Great Vance', a music-hall performer who sang a song called *Walking in the Zoo on Sunday*:

> *The Stilton, Sir, the Cheese, the OK thing to do*
> *On Sunday afternoon is to toddle in the Zoo ...*[2]

Land on the north side of the Regent's Canal was reacquired in 1869, but the full extent of the North Gardens was not used until 1905–6 [**Plans 2** and **3**].

No buildings survive from the early Victorian period, a time when the new installations were notable for their functional innovation. A Carnivora Terrace was built in 1843 with a Mr Elmslie, probably Edmund Wallace Elmslie, as the architect. The world's first Reptile House opened in 1849 [**5**] and the Fish House, the first public marine aquarium, followed in 1853, the latter with

5 The world's first Reptile House, 1849 (from The Illustrated London News, *2 June 1849).*

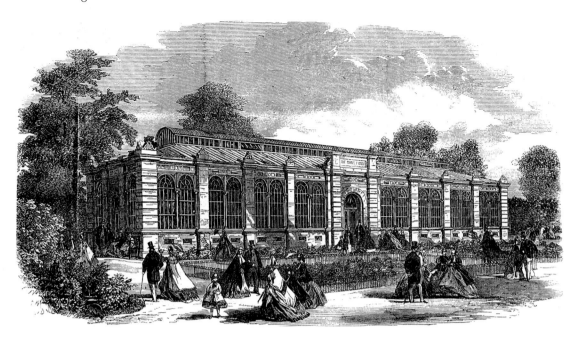

Anthony Salvin junior

6 *The Monkey House, 1864; Anthony Salvin junior, architect (from* The Illustrated London News, *23 July 1864).*

table-top tanks designed by Philip Henry Gosse. These were functional sheds where, the animals aside, attention focused on the methods, rather than the trappings, of display. The availability of large panes of plate glass was an important factor. Regent's Park remained innovative in the display of smaller animals, introducing the world's first insect house, an iron and glass structure, in 1881.

Dominant figures at the Victorian Zoo were Philip Lutley Sclater, Secretary to the Zoological Society from 1859 to 1903, and Abraham Dee Bartlett, Superintendent of the Gardens from 1859 to 1897. Bartlett took a hand in the design of buildings, but this work fell principally to Anthony Salvin junior (1827–81), a Fellow of the Zoological Society and Architect to the Zoo from 1859 to 1878. Salvin was responsible for a number of large new buildings, of which only two survive, the African (formerly Eastern) Aviary of 1864 [**74**, **75** and **76**] and the Parrot House (formerly Refreshment Rooms) of 1868–78 [**100** to **104**]. Salvin also designed an Antelope House (1859–61), a Monkey House (1864) [**6**], an Elephant and Rhinoceros House (1868–9) [**7**] and a Lion House (1875–7) [**8**]. George Smith and Company, building contractors associated with the Salvin family, were frequently employed.

The Eastern Aviary, the Lion House and the Monkey House are loosely classical in style. The latter, a 'conservatory' with an iron and glass roof, was still very much a garden building. The Elephant and Rhinoceros House and Parrot House are in a style that is a clumsy engrossment of Burton's original *cottage orné* approach. Salvin was eclectic but unimaginative; in the words of his father's biographer, a 'dismal talent'.[3] His buildings do not stand up well to comparison with contemporary zoo architecture elsewhere. Berlin, for example, had a spectacular array of exotic animal houses. Some projects, for example the Lion House, did

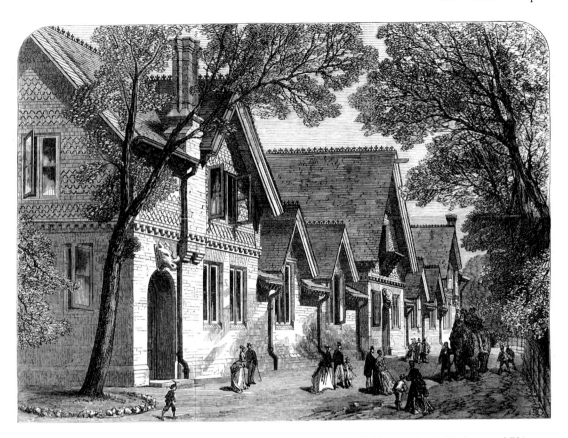

encompass sideways glances to Continental zoos, but building work at Regent's Park seems generally to have been undertaken within a fairly narrow frame of reference. The layout of the gardens was deromanticised and domesticated; Burton's irregularity gradually disappeared in favour of straight walks and four-square buildings of relatively conventional appearance. This may simply reflect Salvin's limitations as an architect, though it could also be

7 The Elephant and Rhinoceros House, 1869; Anthony Salvin junior, architect (from The Illustrated London News, *26 June 1869).*

8 The Lion House, built 1875–7; Anthony Salvin junior, architect. View from the north taken in 1974 (Zoological Society of London photograph).

Charles Brown Trollope

interpreted as an expression of a collective desire for a 'tame' context within which to view the wild beasts.

From about 1882 to 1903 building works were under the supervision of Charles Brown Trollope (d 1903), a founding partner of Widnell and Trollope, quantity surveyors. Trollope had qualified as an engineer; as an architect he was competent but not distinguished. His Bird (formerly Reptile) House of 1882–3 [17 to 20] is an industrial shed in French Renaissance fancy dress, built with a Parisian equivalent in mind. The wide-span roof displays his talents more than the elevations. The Stork and Ostrich House of 1896–7 [21 to 24] was also built to Trollope's designs, here in a low-key domestic revival style. The roofing again betrays the engineering background of the architect. The basic form of the building – a long rectangle with a central gabled cross range – follows that of Salvin's Antelope House, which stood on an adjoining site.

Heating and ventilation

As huts, paddocks and cages gave way to large and relatively complicated animal houses the architectural problems posed by the requirements of animal display had to be tackled. Heating was a major consideration if tropical animals were to be accommodated in the English climate. The earliest animal houses were crudely heated. The Giraffe House had a system supplied by Charles Sylvester, a London heating engineer, author of *The Philosophy of Domestic Economy* (1819) and designer of a hot-air heating system based on that invented by William Strutt of Belper. By the 1830s hot-water heating systems had come to be recognised as more efficient than hot-air systems[4] so were preferred in later Zoo buildings. From 1849 the display of reptiles, amphibians and fish was also dependent on effective heating. Cold-blooded animals need warmth to be active, and thereby interesting to view. However, the Zoo's heating systems were inflexible and resulted in stuffy, overheated interiors.

The challenge was to provide different levels of heat for the animals and for the people who came to view them. The 1882–3 Reptile House attempted to confine the heat from its original hot-water heating system to the cages by running the pipes immediately under their raised slate floors. South skylighting and a closed porch were designed to keep the public areas warm rather than hot. This did not work as intended, however, since there was still no reliable way of regulating the heat. The Stork and Ostrich House was divided longitudinally so that each half could be kept at a different temperature. It retains hot-water pipes along its spine wall. Heat was conserved by the use of closed porches and an unfenestrated north wall.

Ventilation was a related concern. Vitiated air was a Victorian obsession as it was widely believed that disease was transmitted through bad air. Those animal houses that were entered by the public therefore held enormous potential for concern. In the 1860s the early enclosures were criticised as 'stifling and ill-smelling'.[5] The Antelope House, with vent dormers, and the high-roofed Elephant and Rhinoceros House were designed with ventilation as a leading consideration.

As the Zoo gained in popularity, and open-air enclosures were superseded by animal houses with internal public viewing areas, the control of public circulation became a problem. Salvin's animal houses were long rectangles, some with closed end porches. Axial passages, sometimes broadened into halls, overlooked linear series of dens. The 1882–3 Reptile (now Bird) House is a large hall with generous circulation space, originally including three ponds in the floor. The Stork and Ostrich House disciplines circulation by means of a refinement of the linear range; corridors either side of a spine wall allow there-and-back perambulation.

The most basic design requirement, the prevention of escape, was addressed directly. Animals were separated from the public by iron bars or, where such would not serve, plate glass. Service spaces were provided, keepers generally using passages behind the dens. The Elephant and Rhinoceros House even had upper-storey bedrooms for its attendants. The 1882–3 Reptile House has narrow service passages on three sides from which simple timber doors serve the cages. However, no thought seems to have been given to built-in protection from the poisonous snakes.

The conditions and context of animal display were not major considerations in the early Zoo. Monkey poles and a Bear Pit [9], forms of display that would now be thought barbaric, were regarded as perfectly acceptable. Burton's 'follies' may have been less cruel and more decorative, but they show little regard for the animals' welfare or their appropriate display. The purpose-built animal houses of the later 19th century were generally conceived as improvements resulting in a more 'natural' environment for the animals, for: 'We are all tired of the dismal menagerie cages. The cramped walk, the weary restless movement of the head ...'.[6]

As early as 1849 the Reptile House was said to 'reproduce, as far as can be done by artificial means, the natural conditions of reptilian existence'.[7] The Monkey House of 1864 was designed as a conservatory 'to reproduce as nearly as maybe the circumstances under which its occupants live in their native haunts'.[8] The 1875–7 Lion House was expressly designed to display animals in 'a state of nature'. Its outside cages, measuring 20 ft by 12 ft (6 m by 3·5 m), were a spacious improvement on previous arrangements and were originally landscaped with rockwork, yet to our eyes they seem confining and prison-like. Though the claims made for these buildings may now seem ludicrous, there were no precedents and little capacity for the simulation of animal habitats, of which knowledge was in any case limited.

The introduction of 'nature' into animal display – and at this stage that meant, primarily, providing greater space – heightened the dramatic effect, since animals are more entertaining on a bigger stage. However, the reputation of the Victorian Zoo as a peepshow is not entirely deserved. For many of those most closely

Circulation

Natural display

9 The Bear Pit in 1832 (from C F Partington, National History and Views of London, 1832, drawn by T H Shepherd, engraved by J Shury).

involved, the improvements were motivated by the perception that the animals' health and 'happiness' mattered, whether for science or conscience. In 1887 the President of the Zoological Society said of the Zoo's animals: 'the more they are surrounded by conditions reproducing those of their native haunts, the happier they will be ... Much as has been done in this direction, we must all admit that there is still more required. The buildings of today will, we may even hope, some day seem to our successors what the former ones seem to us.'[9]

1900 to 1945

Peter Chalmers Mitchell

In 1902 the Zoological Society of London formed a Committee of Re-organisation and, a year later, in a contested election, Sir Peter Chalmers Mitchell CBE FRS (1864–1945) was appointed Secretary, a post he held until 1935.[10] Mitchell is a key figure in the subsequent history of the development of London Zoo. He was a reformer who actively oversaw much new building, ranging from the Mappin Terraces to the Penguin Pool. He encouraged innovative and less insular approaches to animal display, urging, in particular, better open-air facilities for the animals.

Development plan

Anticipating a large programme of new works, Continental zoos were examined, and then, in 1909, Mitchell brought in John James Joass (1868–1952), junior partner in the firm Belcher and Joass, to draw up a general plan for future development. This was the first such plan since 1827, and Joass's arrival was the Zoo's first decisive move involving the architectural profession since Burton's employment. The plan recommended maximum open-air for the animals with improved facilities and circulation for visitors. A considerable expansion was proposed, but in 1911 this was rejected by the Crown Commissioners.

The Joass plan had a controversial reception within the Zoo. Captain George Swinton, Chairman of the London County Council, was brought on to the Society's Garden Committee in 1912 to develop the scheme.[11] He masterminded a grandiose plan for the Zoo, published in 1913, that proposed obliterating what remained of Burton's informal layout. The area south of the East Tunnel was to have a large open court with three large buildings on its north side looking down a long axial walk. War intervened and much of the scheme remained unexecuted. Some components – the West Tunnel and the open court with a tea-house and restaurant (the Pavilion and Regent Buildings) – were built in the 1920s, thus improving circulation and catering.

Expansion

Much growth took place outside the parameters of the Swinton scheme with funds for development and maintenance coming, as they always had, from gate money, the Society's subscriptions and occasional benefactions. A sanatorium was built in 1908–9; an adjoining prosectorium (dissecting room) survives. In 1909–10 the

Zoological Society moved its offices and library from Hanover Square to Regent's Park, into a new building designed by Joass [112, 113 and 114]. The Zoo expanded to the south in 1908 with the acquisition of what were called the Park Paddocks. An area of new land to the west was also taken in, for the building of the Mappin Terraces, in 1913–14. Further expansion within Regent's Park was ruled out, although in 1935 the Zoo did extend on to land to the east up to the Broad Walk (the Wolf Wood area), this addition bringing it up to its present size of 36 acres (14·4 ha) [10 and Plan 3]. The opening in 1931 of the Zoological Society's gardens at Whipsnade, Bedfordshire, provided an opportunity for further growth on another site.

In 1935 London Zoo formed the first children's zoo in Britain, with German precedent as the model. It began as 'Pet's Corner', on the Fellows' Lawn near the Regent Building, and was intended to give urban children, for whom close contact with animals was otherwise rare, an opportunity to touch or handle young or domesticated specimens. In 1938, in a ceremony performed by the young Edward and Robert Kennedy, the Children's Zoo proper opened on its present site, part of what had been the Park Paddocks. The Zoo remained open through World War II. There was considerable bomb damage, though only the Zebra House was wholly destroyed. The tunnels were used as air-raid shelters.

Through the early part of the century, building design was, in the main, directly overseen by the Society's zoologists, led by Mitchell. In fact the Mappin Terraces [55 to 63], the Insect House of 1912–13 [25] and, quite probably, the Sea Lion Pond of 1905 [82] were basically designed by him. The 1923–4 Aquarium [57 and 66 to 71], under the Mappin Terraces, was laid out following prescriptions from Mitchell and E G Boulenger. The latter, at first Curator of Reptiles and later Director of the Aquarium, had visited several Continental aquariums to consult experts before determining what was wanted in London.

Zoologists and building design

10 Aerial view of London Zoo from the south in 1935 or thereabouts (NMR/APU TQ 2883/1).

The building of the Reptile House of 1926–7 [**26** to **30**] was closely controlled by Joan Beauchamp Procter (1897–1931), Curator of Reptiles, who had also been actively involved in the landscaping of the Aquarium tanks. For the Reptile House she prepared not only a brief but also the plan, and worked on landscaping the enclosures.[12] David Seth-Smith (1875–1963), a curator trained as an engineer and architect (but perhaps best known as the 'Zoo Man' of the BBC's *Children's Hour* programme), was involved in several works, including the conversion of the 1882–3 Reptile House to a Bird House in 1927–8. The Gorilla House of 1932–3 [**31** to **34**] and Penguin Pool of 1934 [**83** to **86**] were designed to briefs provided by Mitchell, Seth-Smith and Dr Geoffrey Marr Vevers (1890–1970), Superintendent from 1923 to 1948.[13]

Architects

Important though zoologists were to these building projects, architects were responsible for much of the Zoo's raised profile through the early 20th century. Standards of design were markedly better than they had been in the 19th century because architects of high professional standing – notably Joass, Sir Edward Guy Dawber (1862–1938; President of the Royal Institute of British Architects in 1925–7), and the architectural firm called Tecton – were given multiple commissions. Lesser figures were also employed on an occasional basis; the Zoo had no staff architects.

The firm of Belcher and Joass has taken credit for certain works at the Zoo, but John Belcher was in poor health from 1909 and all the firm's Zoo work can be confidently attributed to the junior partner. Joass had been responsible for designing Mappin and Webb Limited's Oxford Street building in 1906–8 and it was he who introduced John Newton Mappin to Peter Chalmers Mitchell as the benefactor for a 'panorama'. The Mappin Terraces were an extraordinary project and (alongside Mitchell and Joass) the engineer, Alexander Drew, and the contractor, D G Somerville and Company, must take credit for what is a *tour de force* of reinforced-concrete construction. Joass's very personal neo-mannerist style, crisp, linear, sparing and precise, found expression in the offices and library of 1909–10 and, to a lesser degree, in the external elevations of the Aquarium of 1923–4. The internal arrangements of the Aquarium presented peculiar difficulties; G Topham Forrest, Chief Architect to the London County Council, 'took a personal interest in helping us through the London Building Acts, the provisions of which covered an Aquarium only uneasily'.[14]

Elsewhere at the Zoo Joass employed a light Italianate style that may have been intended to reflect the approach adopted by Burton. This style is manifested in the Mappin Café of 1920 [**64** and **65**] (first designs 1913), the Pavilion Building of 1921–2 [**105**] and the Regent Building of 1928–9 [**106**, **107** and **108**] (first designs 1914–15). Dawber took the style from Joass and gave it a bit more pomp in the Reptile House of 1926–7 and the Main Gate of 1928 [**90**].

11 The Studio of Animal Art, 1937 (demolished 1962); Tecton, architects (RCHME, H Felton).

Tecton, the modernist architectural firm founded in 1932 and led by Berthold Lubetkin (1901–90), gained its first work at the Zoo. The introduction came through Solly Zuckerman, a Research Anatomist at Regent's Park from 1928 to 1932, who was acquainted with Godfrey Samuel (1904–83), one of the firm's partners. Tecton's first building was the convertible Gorilla House of 1932–3, followed by the Penguin Pool of 1934, early and seminal works of International Modern architecture in Britain.[15] A measure of their architectural radicalism comes through when these buildings are compared with the Reptile House of a few years earlier. Their success brought Tecton further Zoo commissions. In 1936 the firm was responsible for the North Gate Kiosk [**92**], and, in 1937, for the Studio of Animal Art (formerly on the site of the Nuffield Building) [**11**]. A plan for an Elephant House was abandoned because of the outbreak of war. In addition to its work at London Zoo, Tecton designed a number of buildings for Whipsnade Park in 1934–6 and for Dudley Zoo in 1935–7.

Tecton's Regent's Park buildings were not part of a programme or redevelopment scheme; they were taken on one at a time as separate commissions. At the outset the architects seem not to have had a doctrine of zoo architecture as such, though Lubetkin did arrive at what he termed a 'geometric method'; this he defined as 'designing architectural settings for the animals in such a way as to present them dramatically to the public, in an atmosphere comparable to that of a circus'.[16] Others have variously interpreted the buildings as reflections of an exploration of man's place in nature, and as polemical models for what an approach to architecture for human habitation might be. Tecton's approach was basically that of early modernism generally: functionalism through meticulous attention to the brief and 'honest' expression of materials. Formal inventiveness was meant to arise from functional requirements and, in large measure, it did – as, for example, in the circular plan of the Gorilla House [**33**] or the ramps of the Penguin Pool [**85** and **86**]. For Lubetkin, however, architectural design transcended functionalism. He sought visual effect through bold curves and Constructivist sculpture was clearly a reference point if not a source. Ornament and 'style' were not banished. That there is a nod towards Regent's Park neo-classicism in the treatment of the external walls of the Gorilla House seems to be affirmed by the deliberate positioning of a Corinthian capital near the entrance.

Hagenbeckian naturalism

The calls for the introduction of nature into animal display that echoed through the late 19th century were given focus in the early years of the 20th century. Carl Hagenbeck introduced new principles, breaking down the impact of barriers by eliminating visible caging and actually simulating nature in landscaped 'panoramic' enclosures. His ideas were principally expressed through his Tierpark at Stellingen, near Hamburg, opened in 1906. The naturalistic approach was adopted at other zoos in Paris, Cologne, Antwerp and London, where it meshed with Mitchell's commitment to air and freedom for the animals. The Sea Lion Pond of 1905 was London Zoo's first 'natural' enclosure with an artificial cliff providing the backdrop to an islanded pond. The adjoining and contemporary Southern Aviary was a bird enclosure of unprecedented size, to allow relatively free flight. The Prairie Marmot Enclosure (formerly the Coypu Pond) of 1912–13 was novel for the absence of fencing.

The Mappin Terraces

The Mappin Terraces of 1913–14 are the major example of Hagenbeckian naturalism at London Zoo. They consist of a panoramic tiered quadrant for open-air display, topped by artificial hills. Mitchell devised the layout having seen other panoramas. Hagenbeck had erected one in Hamburg in 1907, but another in Antwerp was a more direct model. The Mappin Terraces, though criticised as an 'uncouth mountain range',[17] were generally well received because they were seen as providing improved conditions for deer, bears and goats and a naturalistic and picturesque out-of-doors setting where bars did not intrude between the public and the animals. According to a report in *The Times*: 'One feels that [one] is nearer to and more intimate with [the bears] than has ever before been possible.'[18] London's only previous exhibition of large animals not behind cage bars had come in the form of a temporary 'Wonder Zoo' at Olympia.

The bear enclosures were a vast improvement on the small cages of the Carnivora Terrace and it was supposed that the goats would be more vigorous and healthy on the hills than they could be on level ground. The Monkey Hill, a rock-like mound built in 1924–5 to the west of the Mappin Terraces, was considered such a convincing replication of a natural environment that it was used as a basis for the study of animal behaviour in the wild.[19] It is ironic, and indicative of changing attitudes, that the Mappin Terraces have since come to be viewed as representing some of the worst aspects of enclosing animals for public display. The hills now seem decidedly barren and the high-walled, concrete-surfaced bear enclosures little better than 'bear pits'. Wildlife has become so accessible through television and tourism that it is difficult to imagine how remote was experience of exotic animals in a natural setting from the lives of most Edwardian Londoners.

Simulation of nature was also applied to the indoor display of smaller animals. The Aquarium tanks of 1923–4 were given elaborate rockwork and the Reptile House cages of 1926–7 were fastidiously landscaped, their back walls illusionistically painted by a theatrical scene artist as continuations of rockwork and planting. Such attempts to create an impression of nature clearly benefit the viewer more than the animal. Hagenbeckian naturalism did undoubtedly bring some improvement in conditions for animals. It was, however, based on the spectator's viewpoint, working on the premise that an illusion of free animals in a natural setting is more enjoyable than a view of caged animals. The escape to an unfamiliar world that is part of the experience of any zoo was made more complete and, to the extent that it was ever troubled, the conscience was eased. This is not to suggest that Hagenbeckian naturalism was cynical. Rather it was romantic and unscientific, and involved little serious analysis of animal needs or natural environments.

The lighting of animal houses was given particular attention at London Zoo in the early part of this century. No special lighting seems to have been used in the Zoo's 19th-century buildings; skylighting over the public areas was the rule. Mitchell introduced a method of lighting known as the 'aquarium principle'. The aquarium as a building type had developed in the late 19th century on the Continent and elsewhere in Britain, for example in Brighton. In some aquariums the exhibits were lit from above and the public passages were darkened so that visitors received light only through the tanks.

This theatrical approach was introduced at London Zoo in the Insect House and Small Mammal House of 1912–13 after Mitchell had seen 'aquarium principle' lighting in use at the Small Mammal House in Washington, DC. The Insect House has exhibits flanking a public passage under three separate roofs. The exhibits are skylit and the passage unlit so that light comes to the visitor through the exhibits. Mitchell believed this kind of lighting to be good for the animals as well as engaging for visitors. The approach was used again in the Aquarium in 1923–4 to bring the fish into prominence. Artificial light filters through the tanks to viewers in dark circulation areas.

Indoor display

'Aquarium principle' lighting

15

Circulation

Mitchell prescribed 'aquarium principle' lighting again for the Reptile House of 1926–7. Here there is skylighting over the service areas and the cages. The public areas are not only unlit but were originally made even darker through being painted in shining black. The lighting and the illusionistic landscaping gave visitors the effect of 'a series of magic casements opening onto tropical scenes'.[20]

Logistical problems associated with animal display were also being addressed. Growing crowds on weekends and holidays made circulation increasingly difficult. The Mappin Terraces addressed this with spacious paths on multiple levels. These gave views both up and down, the views downward being originally through openings in walls that obscured visitors above from visitors below.

The Reptile House has a highly considered and practical design. Circulation is regulated through a plan that enforces a there-and-back circuit. Its servicing and security are neatly arranged. There are perimeter cages with outer service passages and a central island with a separate service area. All the dangerous animals are kept in the central island so that if any escape they can be trapped in the enclosed service area. The most dangerous and fast-moving snakes are further confined by the use of high-level doors between the cages and the service area. An upper section originally housed a laboratory and sanatorium.

The Gorilla House presented a radically new approach to circulation. In summer, the gorillas had access to an open-air cage; in winter this outdoor cage was converted to an enclosed public viewing area by means of a retractable wall and roof. The retractable roof pivoted around a central steel column, dictating the building's circular plan [33]. This convertible system was good for the gorillas and it avoided a problem previously encountered: the fact that animals became invisible to the public when they retreated from their open summer cages to their covered winter quarters. The system proved technically awkward, however, and this solution was not used elsewhere.

Technology

Science and technology were increasingly influential on the design of Zoo buildings. Zoological research brought ever more sophisticated understanding of the needs of the animals and technological advances made meeting these within the Zoo increasingly possible. Heating and ventilating systems were vastly improved. The Aquarium has plant to maintain stable temperatures at various levels to suit different species, as well as to maintain water aeration and saline balance. An experimental Monkey House of 1926 combined free access to the open air for the animals with individually heated dens and artificial sunlight from quartz incandescent globes. The Reptile House was the most technologically advanced building of its type in the world when it opened. It incorporated electrical heating with separately controlled thermostats for each cage. In addition the animals were given exposure to ultraviolet light.

Mitchell's emphasis on the importance of fresh air to the animals, particularly large mammals, was reflected in the Gorilla

House. It incorporated an air-conditioning system designed to ensure a controlled indoor climate for its sensitive inhabitants. They were provided with circulating warm humidified air without any sacrifice of display or public comfort. A south-facing clerestory also helped to keep the gorillas healthy. Another example of the application of technology to animal display came in 1936 at the Bird House with what was claimed as the first use at any zoo of non-reflecting glass.

The introduction and acceptance of Tecton's modernist functionalism in the early 1930s seems to reflect a self-conscious desire on the part of the Zoo to express scientific knowledge and technological capabilities in architectural terms. It is fitting that Zuckerman, a scientist, was the intermediary. Of the Gorilla House it was said: 'The double object of science and visibility demanded the simple lines and plain surfaces that have been adopted.'[21] Hagenbeckian naturalism had fallen from favour and Tecton's buildings embodied an attitude to zoo display wherein animal well-being was considered empirically rather than impressionistically. The Penguin Pool may be an abstract Antarctica but it is not a simulacrum. Nature is expressed functionally as a rational order; thus a cantilevered ramp is as 'natural' a habitat as an artificial mountain. A more fundamentally nature-based approach was furthered at Whipsnade where space was less restricted.

Tecton took care to plan and tailor buildings to the specific requirements of the zoologists. The intention was to accommodate the animals' perceived needs, although the primary function of the buildings remained display. This rationalist approach to zoo architecture had no less a sense of theatre than the panoramic approach, which had been criticised because 'it allowed the very shy animals to hide themselves from the public gaze, almost indefinitely, while those with a taste for publicity were not able to indulge it to the best advantage'.[22]

The Gorilla House and Penguin Pool are buildings for exhibits, and frankly so. The floor surfaces of the Gorilla House were designed so that it would be more comfortable for the gorillas to stand near the public than at the back of the cage. The same building's screen wall and sheltered seat overlooking the Regent's Canal are an exhibition-architecture feature that serves as a reminder that this is a garden building. The Penguin Pool was explicitly intended as a showcase for the penguins, 'to exhibit these amusing birds to the best advantage'.[23]

Well received by the architectural profession for its elegance and technical virtuosity, the Penguin Pool has also captured the imagination of a wide public. It can be appreciated simply, as a deliberately contrasting backdrop for the dumpy penguins, or, with a greater and perhaps tendentious regard to the birds' more active moments, as a pointer to the liberating possibilities of modernist architecture. 'How many citizens of London have brooded over the railings of that pool, envying the penguins as they streak through the blue water or plod up the exquisite incline of the ramp – and have wondered sadly why human beings cannot be provided, like the penguins, with an environment so adapted to their needs?'[24] Professor Sir Charles Reilly hoped to 'live long enough to have a small town house, I suppose with one ramp for my wife and another for myself as circumscribed, and complete for my needs, and with no possible addition or alteration – indeed the perfect unity. No doubt I shall have to simplify my habits before I am worthy to live in such a thing of beauty, but that would be very good for me as for most of us.'[25]

1945 to 1992

The 1950–1 Development Plan

Following World War II, the repair and reconstruction of bomb-damaged buildings was a priority. Both the Clock Tower and the Raven's Cage were rebuilt in the late 1940s. An Architect's Department was formed in 1947 under Franz A P Stengelhofen to cope with post-war reconstruction and broader replanning. In 1950 Stengelhofen put forward a Development Plan. This proposed extensive rebuilding with the imposition on the gardens of a formal grid based on the golden section. It introduced moated enclosures and elevated walkways to cope with vast numbers of visitors; in 1950 there were more than 3 million visitors to the Zoo, a figure not subsequently exceeded. The scheme was sanctioned and published in 1951,[26] but no works of consequence ensued because finance for major development was lacking. Little of this plan was ever carried through, though the West Footbridge of 1960–1 [99] does derive from Stengelhofen's proposals for improving circulation.

The 'New Zoo' plan of 1958

The years 1958 to 1976 were a period of intense redevelopment at London Zoo. In 1955 Professor Lord Solly Zuckerman returned to the Zoo as Secretary to the Zoological Society, a post he held until 1977. The well-connected Zuckerman was a facilitator and fund-raiser rather than a reformer like Mitchell. Hopes for a rebuilding of the Zoo were revived in 1956 when Sir Hugh Casson was commissioned to prepare an alternative to the 1951 plan. Casson worked with Stengelhofen and Sir Peter Shepheard was brought in as a landscape consultant. The plan for the 'New Zoo' was published in 1958[27] and it was estimated that up to £3m would be needed for the multi-phase ten-year programme, to be funded from the Society's reserves and benefactions. Numerous new buildings were projected as part of a plan that reverted to the principle of informal grouping. Particular emphasis was laid on improvement of the canal banks and elevated walkways remained an intention. However, the design of particular buildings was left to be addressed by individual architects as occasion required.

Redevelopment

Work on the programme began quickly in 1958 with the erection of new service buildings behind the Mappin Terraces. This made space available for a complete reordering of the west end of the Middle Gardens as the Cotton Terraces of 1960–3 [35 and 36].

12 Aerial view of London Zoo from the south in 1983 (Aerofilms Limited).

Other major buildings for animal display went up in quick succession – the Northern Aviary of 1962–4 [**77** to **81**], the Elephant and Rhino Pavilion of 1962–5 [**37** to **42**] and the Charles Clore Pavilion for Mammals of 1965–7 [**43**, **44** and **45**]. There was then a pause during which the programme was reviewed and financial assistance secured from the Government.[28] Next followed the Michael Sobell Pavilions for Apes and Monkeys of 1970–2 [**46** to **49**], and the New Lion Terraces of 1972–6 [**50** to **54**].

Casson's 1958 plan served throughout as a skeleton and siting guide rather than as a comprehensive vision. The projects, as fleshed out, in fact bore little relation to the 1958 scheme, of which much was left unrealised. Very large areas of the Zoo had been redeveloped without evident co-ordination and without fundamentally changing the layout [**12** and **Plan 4**]. The end of the campaign of reconstruction was marked with the completion of the New Lion Terraces in 1976, the 150th anniversary of the foundation of the Zoological Society of London. Capital expenditure of £4·4m in the period 1961 to 1976 was funded principally through government grants of £2·7m (61 per cent), with private donations accounting for £950,000 (22 per cent) and the Society's reserves for £750,000 (17 per cent).[29]

A secondary, but concurrent, programme of works related to development of the Zoological Society's auxiliary activities at Regent's Park. A new Animal Hospital and Pathology Laboratory was built, well away from public areas, in 1955–6. The Zoo's position as a major centre of zoological research was reinforced through Zuckerman when, in 1961, the Society undertook to

Research facilities

establish new research laboratories. Funding was obtained for two buildings: the Wellcome Institute of Comparative Physiology (Wellcome Building) of 1963, for the study of reproductive physiology, and the Nuffield Institute of Comparative Medicine (Nuffield Building) of 1964–5 [**115**, **116** and **117**], for the study of disease in animals. Support facilities were further improved in 1973–5 with a new building for the Zoo's Education Department, which also incorporated a Centre for Life Studies [**118** and **119**].

Architects

The existence of an Architect's Department from 1947 to 1991 allowed much building design to be handled in-house. Stengelhofen, Staff Architect until 1966, was succeeded by John Toovey, until 1987, then by Colin Wears, until 1991. The major projects of the 1960s were, however, given to prominent outside architects on an *ad hoc* basis. Sir Hugh Casson, Neville Conder and Partners took on the West Footbridge, the Elephant and Rhino Pavilion and the Education Centre. Sir Peter Shepheard stayed on to work on the Cotton Terraces and the landscaping of the rest of the south bank of the canal. Anthony Armstrong-Jones (Lord Snowdon), Cedric Price and Frank Newby, engineer, formed a team to design the Northern Aviary; Llewelyn-Davies, Weeks and Musgrave took on the Nuffield Building and Black, Bayes and Gibson the Clore Pavilion.

Zoologists continued to inform the design of animal buildings. This influence was particularly decisive in the Sobell Pavilions and the New Lion Terraces, where Toovey was the architect in charge and Dr M R Brambell, Curator of Mammals, provided briefs.

Engineers have also played a crucial role in building design at the Zoo. Ove Arup had worked with Tecton, and Newby was a critical contributor to the Northern Aviary. Anthony Hunt Associates were responsible for inventive space-frame roofs in the Sobell Pavilions and, with Ove Arup and Partners, for the tensile tent of the Amphitheatre of 1982–5 [**110**]. R T James and Partners worked on the New Lion Terraces and Whitby and Bird on the African Aviary of 1989–90 [**74**, **75** and **76**].

The 1980s

From the 1960s the Zoo's visitor numbers declined while staffing costs increased. By the 1980s financial problems had become acute. In 1988 a government grant of £10m was given with a stipulation that the Zoological Society set up a subsidiary, Zoo Operations Ltd, to manage the Zoo. The John S Bonnington Partnership, which had designed a zoo in Qatar, was brought in and a major development scheme was promulgated in 1989 with the aim of halting the decline.[30] Initially this proposed a large expansion of the Zoo to the south, but this was blocked by concerted opposition. Plans for four large new exhibition-centre displays, including an overhaul of the Mappin Terraces to form a 'Szechuan Experience' (for the display of giant pandas), had been prepared by Peter Chermayeff of Cambridge Seven Associates, Boston-based architects specialising in zoo work. These remained unfunded but some relatively small projects were completed in 1989–90. The Eastern Aviary was largely rebuilt and renamed the

African Aviary, and Barclay Court [**111**] was formed with a revamped restaurant and new shop, resuscitating the focal point that had been the centrepiece of Swinton's 1913 plan.

In the years around 1960, international orthodoxy in zoo architecture placed a strong emphasis on landscape and the simulation of the animals' natural habitats, an approach perhaps best represented by Milwaukee Zoo where predator and prey are separated only by moats in shared enclosures. In London, however, there was another important thread. Casson's 1958 scheme revived the exhibition-building aesthetic that Tecton had introduced to London Zoo in the 1930s, transmuted through the spirit of the Festival of Britain. Spectacular modernism was again applied to animal display in two buildings that were intended to be dominant features: the Elephant and Rhino Pavilion and the Northern Aviary. The Zoo was hugely popular in the early 1960s as a place to have fun and these buildings express the ethos of public entertainment. The Elephant and Rhino Pavilion is a bold and apposite exercise in New Brutalism; its bulky massing and wrinkled surfaces speak of its inhabitants. Zoomorphism was also applied in the skeletal and apparently airborne Northern Aviary, an early large tension structure that was also pioneering in its use of aluminium. These exotic and contrasting buildings demand attention and are, with the Mappin Terraces and Tecton's work, the principal architectural excitements of the Zoo.

The Elephant and Rhino Pavilion and the Northern Aviary are not, however, purely showpieces. J M Richards praised the former for combining 'the fantastic and the functional'.[31] Its materials, plan and profiles all derive from practical requirements, the surface texturing, for instance, being designed to deter damage by the elephants and rhinoceroses.

The Elephant and Rhino Pavilion also has a distinctive and theatrical application of 'aquarium principle' lighting, a feature also present in the buildings of the Cotton Terraces and the Clore Pavilion. The pens are lit by concealed skylights while the public is kept in a dark timber-ceiled interior to give an impression of 'animals standing in bright top-lit clearings in a forest'.[32]

The 'Moonlight World', in the basement of the Clore Pavilion, was an important innovation in terms of lighting and illusionistic display. The natural rhythms of nocturnal animals are here reversed by artificial lighting so that the lights are off during visiting hours and the animals are active; during the night the lights come on and the animals sleep. The first large-scale exhibit of its kind, it has been widely copied elsewhere.

The effects of lighting can also be seen as aspects of landscaping. As already indicated, this was the paramount design consideration in most of the animal buildings of the 1960s and 1970s, though overshadowed by architectural pyrotechnics in the early 1960s. The Cotton Terraces are, in large measure, landscape architecture. They were laid out with a viewing terrace and paddocks on the canal bank. On the other side of the buildings, which take a low-key architectural tone from Burton's Giraffe House, there are moated paddocks. This was the first use of moats, as a substitute for railings, in London Zoo; the feature was used again at the Elephant and Rhino Pavilion. Landscape was central to the Northern Aviary where the awkward siting on the canal bank contributed to the design. A retaining wall is disguised as a cliff and there is an internal water system with waterfalls. Together with trees and shrubs, these features provide a variety of bird habitats.

In the Sobell Pavilions and the New Lion Terraces 'landscape takes over'.[33] Nature and the open air dominate the buildings in a deliberate echo of the Zoo's original conception as an ornamental garden. The New Lion Terraces are sprawling paddocks, variously landscaped as versions of natural habitats. Concrete screen walls resemble rock outcrops and the moats look like natural ponds. The landscaped enclosures of Whipsnade were a precedent, but the illusion that the animals are in a natural habitat is inevitably constrained by the size of the Regent's Park site. These attempts to break down barriers between animals and visitors, and to simulate nature, represent a revival of Hagenbeck's principles and reflect growing public awareness of 'wildlife'.

Architectural reticence

The dominance of landscape demanded architectural reticence, in part a reaction against the oppressive aspects of earlier animal houses. The Clore Pavilion set the quiet deferential tone, its dark-brown brick forms arranged so as to focus attention on the exhibits. It was praised for leaving visitors 'with a memory of animals and planting rather than of architecture'.[34] This approach was followed in the Sobell Pavilions, where the brown brick blocks are sober, functional and aesthetically modest, aiming for effacement. Attention is directed to the open air, boldly enclosed under space-frame roofs, an unambiguously non-illusionistic version of a natural habitat, in the spirit of the Penguin Pool. Unobtrusiveness was also a guiding principle at the Education Centre. Here the element of animal display was absent, but the objective was to avoid intrusion into the landscape of the gardens. In the New Lion Terraces the buildings are all but lost in the amorphous enclosures. It is not immediately apparent to a visitor that there are any buildings as such in the complex at all.

Circulation

Circulation has been a subject of continuing experimentation. The Elephant and Rhino Pavilion and the Northern Aviary were both innovative. The latter is an early 'walk-through' aviary allowing close-up views of the birds. The Elephant and Rhino Pavilion directs visitors around a subtly arranged S-plan interior in which each pen is separately discovered and low-level viewing areas allow lingering without interfering with the views or movement of others. Circulation is largely undisciplined in the later complexes, which are intended to be environmental, rather than theatrical, experiences. The covered walkways of the Sobell Pavilions and the New Lion Terraces, which have no public interiors at all, are a practical concession to the comfort of outdoor viewers.

The dominance of landscape in the buildings of the 1970s did not come about purely for the sake of display. In part it reflects a growing emphasis on animal welfare. The Sobell Pavilions and the New Lion Terraces were entrusted to staff architects and they are notable for their emphasis on curatorial requirements. The Sobell Pavilions are arranged in such a way that species are screened from each other; for apes and monkeys a degree of privacy was thought to be essential for tranquillity and successful breeding. There are multiple openings between the indoor and outdoor areas specially to prevent dominant animals from controlling the movement of others. For the sake of the animals and their keepers both complexes have non-public indoor cages as well as spacious and well-appointed service areas.

Caging is no longer just an impediment to a view. It is something the public prefers not to know about. Closure of the prison-like viewing passages to the dens on the lower level of the Cotton Terraces reflects this fact as much as it does concern for the welfare of the timid antelopes. Animals such as the bears, which were seen as not being suitably accommodated, have been moved away from the limiting confines of Regent's Park. Animal display has been in retreat, apologetic in the face of broadening antipathy to zoos. An installation within the Sobell Pavilions exemplifies this ambivalence to the viewing of caged animals through a deliberately ironic conservationist message: caging labelled 'Human' is subtitled 'London Zoo presents – The Most Destructive Animal in the World'.

Changing attitudes to zoos notwithstanding, there have been continuing attempts to resolve the conflict between animal needs and the desire of a broad section of the public to see animals naturalistically and entertainingly displayed. The African Aviary of 1990, the first major new exhibit at the Zoo since 1976, is a strikingly engineered showpiece of high-tech design that manages at the same time to be reticent about its presence through the use of wires that are virtually invisible. The enclosures were landscaped by film-set designers to imitate African habitats, recalling the 'magic casements' of the Reptile House. Another example of illusionistic display can be seen in recent exhibits at the Insect House where cockroaches roam a dirty kitchen sink and ants explore an abandoned picnic. Whether realised or not, the plans by Peter Chermayeff for large themed 'naturalistic' exhibits suggest that the simulation of nature endures as an approach to animal display.

The 1990s and beyond

In July 1991 London Zoo announced that its financial position was such that it would have to close in September 1992. Alternatives to closure, based on the 1989 Chermayeff scheme and on a more conservation-minded approach, were subsequently discussed. Closure and large-scale redevelopment were both ruled out in

March 1992, only to resurface as possibilities in June. At the brink, closure was again forestalled, and, in October 1992, a decision was taken to develop the Zoo as a centre for the breeding and conservation of endangered species. At the time of writing the future of the Zoo and its buildings hangs in the balance.

Notes

1 Toovey, J W 1976. '150 years of building at London Zoo'. In S Zuckerman (ed) *Zoological Society of London Symposium: 1826–1976 and Beyond*, p 180.
2 As quoted by Blunt, W 1976. *The Ark in the Park: The Zoo in the Nineteenth Century*, p 29.
3 Allibone, J 1987. *Anthony Salvin: Pioneer of Gothic Revival Architecture*, p 151.
4 Burton, N: unpublished notes on early 19th-century central heating.
5 *Illustrated London News*, 26 June 1869, p 641.
6 *Daily News*, 1869, as quoted by Toovey in Zuckerman 1976, p 179.
7 *Illustrated London News*, 2 June 1849, p 384
8 Sclater, P L 1876. *Guide to the Gardens of the Zoological Society of London*, p 10.
9 Zoological Society of London, *Annual Report*, as quoted by Toovey in Zuckerman 1976.
10 *The Times*, 24 April 1935.
11 Also in 1912 Swinton was appointed to head the Town Planning Committee for New Delhi.
12 A sculpted portrait bust of Miss Procter, by George Alexander, is in the entrance lobby of the Reptile House.
13 The crediting to Professor Sir Julian Huxley, Secretary of the Zoological Society from 1935 to 1942, of the commissioning of the Gorilla House (1932–3) and Penguin Pool (1934) is a canard. Huxley did not have the opportunity to make a significant impact on the fabric of the Zoo before war put a stop to building work.
14 Mitchell, P C 1929. *Centenary History of the Zoological Society of London*, p 172.
15 In 1970 the Gorilla House and the Penguin Pool were amongst the first 1930s buildings to be 'listed'.
16 Lubetkin as quoted in Allan, J 1992. *Berthold Lubetkin: Architecture and the Tradition of Progress*, p 199.
17 *The Times*, 10 April 1914 .
18 Ibid.
19 Zuckerman, S 1932. *The Social Life of Monkeys and Apes*.
20 *The Builder*, 24 June 1927, p 1008.
21 *Architectural Review*, June 1933, p 242.
22 *Architect and Building News*, 1 June 1934, pp 254–5.
23 Huxley, J S 1939. *Official Guide to the Gardens and Aquarium of the Zoological Society of London*, p 56.
24 *Mother and Child*, as quoted by M Reading, *Architect's Journal*, 5 Feb 1992, p 29.
25 *Architect's Journal*, 10 Jan 1935, p 70.
26 *Architect and Building News*, 25 May 1951, pp 591–3.
27 *The Builder*, 20 March 1959, pp 538–9.
28 *Nature*, 25 June 1992, p 621.
29 Zoological Society of London, *Annual Report: 1991–2*, p 26.
30 *Architect's Journal*, 17 May 1989, p 12.
31 *Architectural Review*, July 1965, p 17.
32 *The Builder*, 16 July 1965, p 124.
33 Toovey in Zuckerman 1976, p 194.
34 Ibid.

2

Animal Houses

*The Giraffe House
(BB92/21617).*

Clock Tower

1828, Decimus Burton, architect; clock turret added 1831 and rebuilt 1844. Reconstructed 'in an improved form' 1897–8, Charles Brown Trollope, architect; George Smith and Company, builders. Bomb damaged 1940 and wholly rebuilt 1946–7, Burnet, Tait and Lorne, architects. Converted to chair store in 1958 and shops in 1988. Listed Grade II.

The Clock Tower [**13**, **14**, and **15**] would be the earliest surviving building at the Zoo except that it has twice been rebuilt. Constructed as a 'Gothic House for Lamas', it was soon given over to camels. Early views indicate that it was much more picturesque in its original form and thus characteristic of Burton's early Zoo buildings and of earlier menageries in general.

The east elevation has a mullioned-and-transomed bay window flanked by four-centred arched openings which formerly gave on to a paddock. To the west there was a veranda on rustic timber columns. This and the elaborate bargeboards are absent from the surviving brick, concrete and machine-tiled building, which lacks much of the charm of Burton's original. The basic form is as conceived by Burton, though his clock turret was a simple affair. The design of the ogee-topped copper-clad clock tower dates from 1844.

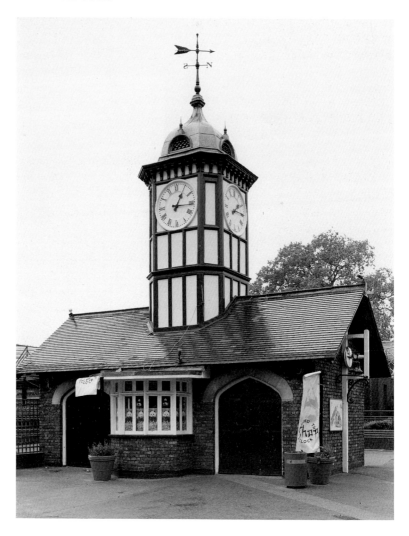

13 The Clock Tower (formerly the Camel House) as rebuilt in 1946–7, viewed from the east (BB92/20472).

14 (Left) The original Camel House (now the Clock Tower) as designed by Decimus Burton, view from the south in 1835 (from a lithograph by G Scharf).

15 (Above) The Camel House showing the clock tower as rebuilt in 1844, view from the north in 1848 (from a lithograph by F W Hulme).

Sources
The Mirror, 6 Sept 1828, p 149; 29 Sept 1832, p 280.
BAL, RIBA Drawings, RAN 30 K/7.

Giraffe House

Plan 4:21

The Giraffe House [**16**] was built as a direct result of the acquisition of the Zoo's first four giraffes, Selim, Mabrouk, Guib-allah and Zaida. It is an emphatically functional shed, a 'Tuscan' barn, without the picturesque flourishes of Burton's earlier Zoo architecture. In most respects unrefined, it was built with a central heating system for the sake of these tropical animals. Its height, about 16 ft (5 m) to the heads of the doors and 21 ft (6·5 m) to the eaves, gives the building its distinction and bears witness to its function.

The central block is a simple stock-brick shed with tall round-headed stable doors, broad five-light windows in the returns and deep modillioned eaves, all original features. However, only the south and return walls survive from the original building. The indoor public viewing and circulation area was formerly in a low north block in which stood slender cylindrical columns, presumably of cast iron.

The central block is flanked by rebuilt low wings. That to the east was the Hippo House from 1850 when Obaysch, the first hippopotamus seen in England, arrived to great public fascination.

The post-war rebuilding, as part of the Cotton Terraces development (*see* below), respects Burton's building. The main block is

1836–7, Decimus Burton, architect. Wings added 1849–50. Bomb-damaged 1940 and largely rebuilt 1960–3, Franz Stengelhofen and Colin Wears, architects. Listed Grade II.

16 The Giraffe House with its 16 ft (5 m) high doors, view from the south east in 1990 (NBR 90/553).

lit at a high level only, with almost continuous north-lights near the eaves. The public viewing area to the north, entered via the wings, is in a deliberately low-lit lean-to, built over a lower ground floor containing toilets and offices. The indoor animal dens have mosaic-tiled walls, the skylit wings housing zebras and okapi. Earlier fences around the paddocks to the south were replaced with moats.

Sources
The Builder, 21 Oct 1960, pp 738–9.
Architect and Building News, 19 Oct 1960, p 487.
Architect's Journal, 20 Oct 1960, p 566.
English Heritage (London Region) photographs.

Bird House
Plan 4:73

1882–3 as a Reptile House, Charles Brown Trollope, architect; Holland and Hannen, builders; cost £9,175. Converted 1927–8, P E C Lain, architect, to a scheme devised by David Seth-Smith, Curator of Birds and Mammals, and a committee of ornithologists.
Small bird aviaries inserted 1974, John Toovey, architect. North service block added.

The Bird House was built as a Reptile House [17 to 20] to replace the 1849 reptile house, the world's first. The 1882–3 Reptile House, a facility rivalled only by that in Paris, was in part funded through the sale to P T Barnum of Jumbo, the Zoo's celebrity elephant. It has grand Second Empire elevations, now largely obscured, with a light interior under wide-span metal-trussed shed roofs. Its original heating system, though ineffective, was designed to confine most of the heat to the cages by means of hot-water pipes running under their floors. The public circulation hall was warmed through south sky-lighting and a large closed entrance porch, the latter originally used for cases displaying small animals, such as frogs and toads, capable of surviving in cooler temperatures.

The main block is a rectangle of about 120 ft (36 m) by 60 ft (18 m). To the south the three centre bays originally projected as a double porch with entrances in the returns. To the north there is a comparable projection for offices. The pilastered elevations, red brick with Corse Hill sandstone dressings, are punctuated by

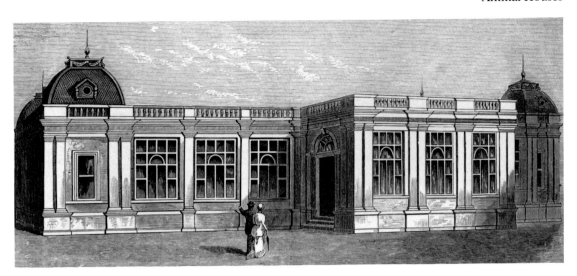

17 (Above) The Bird House (formerly the Reptile House) as built in 1882–3 with funds in part from the sale of Jumbo the elephant (from Zoological Society of London Annual Report 1882/3).

18 (Below) 1927 plan for the conversion of the Reptile House to the Bird House (from Zoological Society of London Architects' Drawings – original in BAL, RIBA Drawings Collection, RAN 30 K/4[1]).

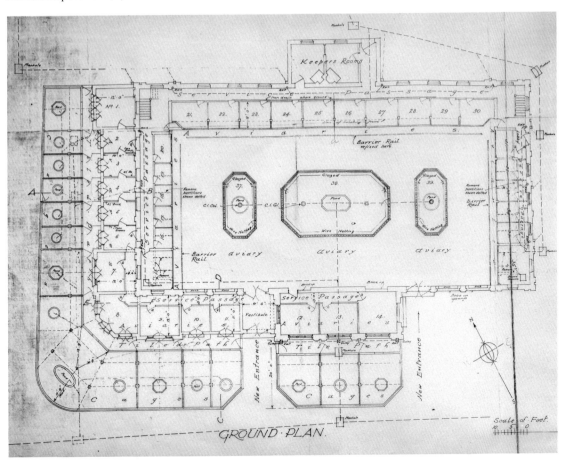

GROUND·PLAN.

19 *The Bird House interior from the south east (BB91/28124).*

corner cupolas (those to the south have been removed) and parapets with terracotta balustrading.

Twin hipped slate roofs rest on wrought-iron trusses with a 25-ft (7·6 m) span, strengthened by 'blocked' (that is composite) struts. The interior is bisected by a row of slender cylindrical cast-iron columns with 'Corinthian' capitals, 14 ft (4·2 m) in height. There were originally ten cages each to the north, east and west, the larger ones to the north for large snakes, the smaller ones for small snakes and lizards. Those to the north have been enlarged into the building, those to east and west rearranged as six to each side. The central circulation hall has a patterned Granolithic floor, originally broken up by three ponds, the larger to the centre for crocodiles. Hanging baskets and potted plants were an important part of the

20 The Bird House interior from the south west (BB91/28123).

original décor. The hall is ringed by the pipes of a secondary heating system.

The conversion to bird display wrecked the external architecture with the addition of brick lean-to aviaries and metal caging to the south and west. The south-west corner has a date plaque and new entrances flank the former porch. An attic laboratory was added to the north, reached from staircases inserted in the angles of the main block.

Sources
BAL, RIBA Drawings, RAN 30 J/1[1] and K/4 (copies held in Zoological Society of London Architects' Drawings).
Illustrated London News, 8 Sept 1883.

21 *The Stork and Ostrich House, built to plans by Charles Brown Trollope in 1896–7, from the south west (BB91/28099).*

Stork and Ostrich House

Plan 4:37

1896–7, Charles Brown Trollope, architect; George Smith and Company, builders; cost £3,788.

The Stork and Ostrich House [**21** to **24**] has been altered very little. It is a long low range in a domestic revival style with pens flanking inner passages to either side of a spine wall. This arrangement, with closed porches at both ends, allowed different temperatures to be maintained in each half of the building. The block was designed for large birds that required protection from the English winter. Hot-water heating pipes survive along the spine wall, heat being conserved by the use of porches and an unfenestrated north wall.

The building is of stock brick with glazed red brick and terracotta dressings, with some rendering and a small timber turret. The door jambs have bullnose bricks, presumably to prevent the animals from injuring themselves on the arrises. Large sliding metal casement windows in the spine wall transmit light to the north half of the building. The pens are 12 ft (3·6 m) deep with

22 *The original 1896 plans for the Stork and Ostrich House showing the longitudinal division to allow differential heating (Zoological Society of London Architects' Drawings – original in BAL, RIBA Drawings Collection, RAN 30 J/I²).*

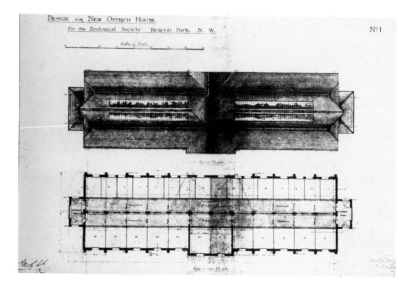

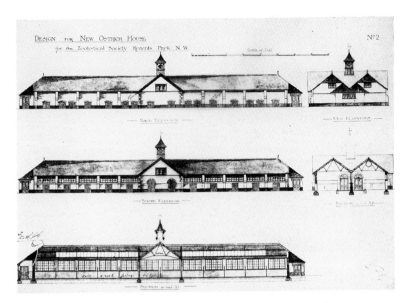

23 The Stork and Ostrich House elevations and sections, 1896 (from Zoological Society of London Architects' Drawings – original in BAL, RIBA Drawings Collection, RAN J/1³).

paddocks extending beyond. The south side was given over to ostriches and other struthious or flightless birds in twelve enclosures. These paddocks were relandscaped in 1992 for other animals. The enclosures on the north side, formerly sixteen latterly eight, remain in the occupation of storks and cranes. The roof has valley skylighting and rests on steel trusses spanning 19 ft 6 in. (5·9 m) with T-section struts and principals. The flooring is of Stuart's patent Granolithic paving.

Sources
BAL, RIBA Drawings, RAN 30 J/1²⁻³ (copies held in Zoological Society of London Architects' Drawings).
Building, 20 April 1979, pp 47–50.

24 The Stork and Ostrich House interior from the south east (BB91/28100).

25 *The Insect House of 1912–13, the first use at the Zoo of 'aquarium principle' lighting; view of the west range from the west (BB92/6333).*

Insect House

Plan 4:15

1912–13, with a £1,500 benefaction from Sir James K Caird; design by Sir Peter Chalmers Mitchell. East range housed small mammals until 1967.

The Insect House [**25**], formerly also a Small Mammal House, replaced a building that had opened in 1881 to house the world's first public display of living insects. It was also the first building at London Zoo to employ 'aquarium principle' lighting, that is, lighting over exhibits on either side of an unlit passage so that light comes to the visitor via the exhibits.

The building has an unembellished stock-brick carcass. It is a reverse L on plan, the two ranges of which were originally quite distinct. The public and display spaces of the west range are raised over a basement housing the Invertebrate Conservation Centre with stores and offices; locusts are bred here for research. Access to the interior is at the west end via a double flight of steps, embracing a large display unit, and a rebuilt porch. There is a triple-span steel-trussed roof with a wide central span over the public passage and smaller spans over the glass-fronted display cases that house insects and a range of other invertebrates. The east range interior, formerly the mammal pens, has been landscaped for an ecological display. Wire-mesh outdoor pens survive on the east side; there were similar pens to the south and west.

Reptile House
Plan 4:36

The Reptile House [**26** to **30**] replaced a building of 1882–3, which was itself a replacement of the world's first reptile house built in 1849 (*see* Bird House above). It was built on the site of an Ape House of 1901–2, parts of which were incorporated. Externally Italianate, in the manner of earlier Zoo buildings by John James Joass, it was designed to a meticulously considered brief and was hailed as the most sophisticated building of its type in the world when it opened. It combined and refined features introduced elsewhere at the Zoo, such as regulated public circulation, differential heating and 'aquarium principle' lighting, whereby the public spaces are purposely dark to highlight animals in landscaped exhibits.

The elevations are of brown Crowborough brick relieved by stucco panels with Spanish green tiled roofs. There are pavilion

1926–7, design by Joan Beauchamp Procter, Curator of Reptiles; Sir Edward Guy Dawber, architect; Prestige and Company, builders; George Alexander, sculptor; original landscaping by John Bull, theatrical scene artist; original heating system devised by the General Electric Company.

26 (Previous page) The Italianate Reptile House of 1926–7, Sir Edward Guy Dawber, architect, viewed from the east (BB91/28078).

27 (Right) Ground-floor plan of the Reptile House as devised by Joan Beauchamp Procter, showing the central island reserved for dangerous animals (based on a plan published in The Architect's Journal, *12 December 1928).*
1 Public Space; 2 Service Areas; 3 Raised Platform; 4 Frog Room; 5 Keeper's Room; 6 Crocodiles; 7 Iguanas; 8 Crocodile Beach; 9 Venomous Snakes; 10 Large Constrictors and Lizards.

28 (Below) The Reptile House, east–west section (from Zoological Society of London Architects' Drawings).

towers and a grand pedimented entrance worthy of a major railway station. As if to counter such a misapprehension the stone door architrave is embellished by finely carved reptiles.

A large rectangular block, the building is entered through a heat-preserving lobby. A wide passage takes visitors round the exhibits and back out of the main entrance. At the inner end there are steps up to a raised platform enclosed by elegant railings with a brass handrail. There were originally sixty-six cages, with dangerous animals all confined to the central island. The outer exhibits have their own service passages. Light comes into the building through steel-trussed roofs over the service areas and cages. Above the south end of the building there is an upper storey built as an

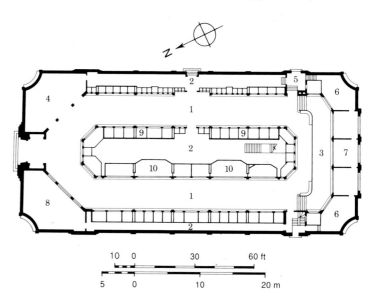

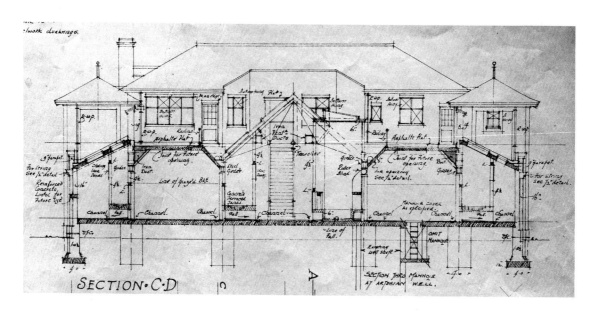

SECTION·C·D

29 (Above) The pedimented main entrance to the Reptile House (BB92/20473).

30 (Left) Detail of the Reptile House main entrance architrave, George Alexander, sculptor (BB92/6335).

infirmary (a precaution against snakebites), laboratory, sanatorium, workshop and office. There are side entrances for staff and to the east an external exhibit cage has been inserted.

Sources

The Times, 15 June 1927.
The Builder, 24 June 1927, pp 1008–9.
Architect's Journal, 21 Dec 1928, pp 837–40.
Bellairs, A d'A and Ball, D J 1976. 'Reptile husbandry today'.
In S Zuckerman (ed) *Zoological Society of London Symposium: 1826–1976 and Beyond*, pp 121–4.

Gorilla House

Plan 4:17

1932–3, brief by Sir Peter Chalmers Mitchell, Secretary, and Dr Geoffrey Marr Vevers, Superintendent; Tecton (Berthold Lubetkin and Godfrey Samuel), architects; Christiani and Nielsen Limited (Ove Arup, Chief Engineer), builders; revolving wall and roof made by J and E Hall Limited; cost £4,060. Altered 1955 and later. Listed Grade I.

31 (Above) The Gorilla House, view from the south when opened in 1933, with the revolving half drum in its winter position (RCHME, H Felton).

The Gorilla House [**31** to **34**] was Tecton's first building anywhere and, though altered, it remains an important example of early modernist architecture in Britain. Although the architects' approach to the building was uncompromisingly functional, the result is a composition that appears sculptural in its apparent formal freedom.

The initiative for the Gorilla House followed the acquisition of two young Congolese gorillas, Mok and Moina. Tecton was introduced via Solly Zuckerman, then a Research Anatomist at the Zoo and a friend of Godfrey Samuel, one of the firm's partners. Sir Peter Chalmers Mitchell suggested a building with convertible open caging to allow the gorillas fresh air in the summer and the public the opportunity to see them in the winter. To meet this complex brief Tecton carried out extensive technical research and negotiated the details with Zoo staff. The heating and ventilating systems, in particular, were carefully designed to ensure a controlled climate. Protection from the elements and from human germs in cold weather were important for the health of the gorillas.

The main block is circular in plan. The northern half, the winter cage, is a walled den lit by a south clerestory to maximise

warmth and light. Heat is conserved by means of a cellular (aerated) concrete lining to the reinforced concrete and by cork insulation in the roof. The southern half was convertible from an open-air cage in the summer to an enclosed public viewing area in the winter. The conversion was achieved by means of a revolving steel and timber screen wall and roof that was hidden inside the north wall in summer. This half drum pivoted around a central steel column (4 in./10 cm in diameter) to enclose the southern semicircle in winter, moving on rollers on a high-level steel track inside steel-frame caging. A glass screen slid across the diameter of the circle to complete the conversion.

Externally, the north wall is articulated by the breaks, like channelled rustication, between the concrete 'lifts'. These horizontal lines are emphasised by the lines of the impressions from the recessed pour joints in the shuttered concrete. The west entrance porch was originally top-lit through round lights, 8 in. (20 cm) in diameter. A screen wall leads to a sheltered seat overlooking the Regent's Canal. The east entrance is more simply treated. The external walls, excepting the porch interiors, have always been white, but the winter cage interior was yellow and blue to suggest openness.

32 The Gorilla House, view from the south in 1992 with the half drum fixed and its cladding removed (BB92/21606).

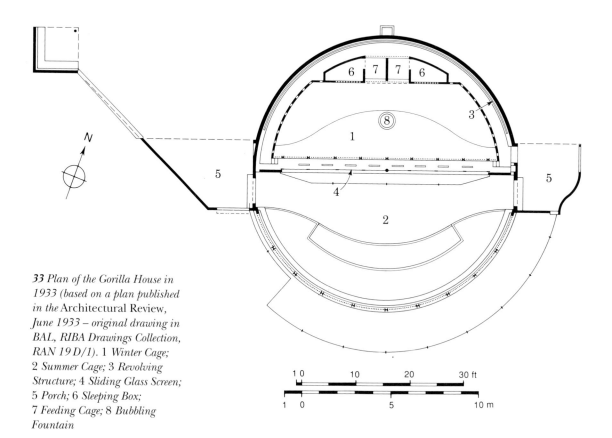

33 Plan of the Gorilla House in 1933 (based on a plan published in the Architectural Review, June 1933 – original drawing in BAL, RIBA Drawings Collection, RAN 19 D/1). 1 Winter Cage; 2 Summer Cage; 3 Revolving Structure; 4 Sliding Glass Screen; 5 Porch; 6 Sleeping Box; 7 Feeding Cage; 8 Bubbling Fountain

34 The Gorilla House, detail of the shuttered concrete north wall showing the channels between the concrete 'lifts' and the articulation of the pour joints (BB92/6400).

The steel frame of the revolving half drum has now been fixed in its winter position and the cladding removed. Steel beams have been inserted to strengthen the summer cage roof. In 1939 the building was adapted to house an elephant and then, in 1955, to house Kodiak bears. It was used for chimpanzees from 1963 and as a breeding colony for apes until 1990 when use of the southern half was abandoned and a koala exhibit was formed, only to be closed in 1992. A public viewing area was formed within a corridor inserted between the entrance porches, using brick walling and conventional glass screens.

Sources

BAL, RIBA Drawings, RAN 19 D/1, RAN 30 L/1.

Architectural Review, June 1933, pp 241–5.

Architect and Building News, 2 June 1933, pp 257–8.

Architect's Journal, 5 Feb 1992, pp 28–37.

Allan, J 1992. *Berthold Lubetkin: Architecture and the Tradition of Progress*, pp 202–8.

Coe, P and Reading, M 1981. *Lubetkin and Tecton: Architecture and Social Commitment*, p 111.

Cotton Terraces

Plan 4:20–23

The Cotton Terraces form the west section of the Middle Gardens, standing on the south bank of the Regent's Canal. The site, excepting the Giraffe House (*see* above), is treated here as a unity. The Cotton Terraces were the first major project to result from the 1958 redevelopment scheme. They accommodate ungulates (hoofed mammals) – camels, deer, antelopes, cattle, horses and giraffes. The architecture, which is simple and unassuming, is designed to be in keeping with Decimus Burton's Giraffe House [**Plan 4:21**] and to make the most of the landscape potential of the canal bank.

A lower terrace running alongside the canal comprises four narrow paddocks [**Plan 4:23**] for deer and antelope [**35 and 36**]. The upper terrace is a railed walkway overlooking these paddocks and linking three animal houses. Indoor accommodation for the deer and antelope is tucked away under projections of the upper terrace, with two rows of six mosaic-tiled dens lit and ventilated through tall concrete shafts which also house service hoists. There are stairs from the upper terrace down to viewing passages for the deer and antelope dens.

1960–3, following a benefaction of £250,000 from Jack Cotton; Franz Stengelhofen and Sir Peter Shepheard, architects (Margaret Maxwell, assistant architect); F J Samuely and Partners, consulting engineers.

35 The Cotton Terraces from the north east (BB92/6322).

To the south two identical brown stock-brick faced buildings stand either side of the Giraffe House, the eastern one for camels and llamas [**Plan 4:20**], the western one for horses and cattle [**Plan 4:22**]. There are concrete plinths and cornices and recessed round-headed north and south entrances with blue mosaic-tile tympana. Internally, there are spacious central public viewing areas interrupted only by slender columns. The perimeter dens have raised floors, mosaic-tiled walling and skylights in the inner slopes of hipped quadrangular roofs, for 'aquarium principle' lighting. There are small service areas at the angles and, outside the buildings, there are moated paddocks [**16**].

Sources

36 The Cotton Terraces, viewing passages for the deer and antelope dens (BB92/6313).

Architect and Building News, 19 Oct 1960, p 487.
The Builder, 21 Oct 1960, pp 738–9.
Architect's Journal, 20 Oct 1960, pp 558, 566.

Elephant and Rhino Pavilion

Plan 4:39

The Elephant and Rhino Pavilion [**37** to **42**] was built as a successor to Anthony Salvin junior's Elephant and Rhinoceros House of 1868–9 [**7** and **Plan 2:7**]. Plans for a new building had been prepared by Tecton in 1939, but the outbreak of war prevented their implementation. The site was chosen in 1950 and the building became the principal southern focus of Casson's 1958 redevelopment plan.

The resulting building could not have formed a greater contrast to its 'Swiss chalet' predecessor. Its style can be characterised as zoomorphic New Brutalism, marvellously expressive of its inhabitants. Despite its dramatic exhibitionism, little about the building is not functionally justified. Textured concrete walls over curved brick plinths, for example, prevent the animals from damaging the fabric.

The main walls are in differing grades of vertically rilled reinforced concrete, hand-hacked to expose the aggregate, with no disguising of the 'lifts'. There are tall copper-felt covered vent and

1962–5, brief by Desmond Morris, Curator of Mammals; Sir Hugh Casson, Neville Conder and Partners, architects; John Mowlem and Company Limited, building contractors. Paddock pool added 1971. Rhino moat altered 1988.

***37** (Above) The zoomorphic architecture of the Elephant and Rhino Pavilion (BB92/21620).*

38 The Elephant and Rhino Pavilion, plan and section in 1965 (from the Architectural Review, *July 1965).*

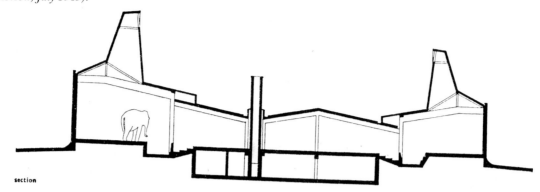

section

key

1. ramp from service yard	4. staff lavatories	7. animal ditches	10. sick bays	13. main rising ducts
2. service yard	5. public entrance	8. rhino pens	11. pen lobbies	14. elephant pool
3. staff mess room	6. store	9. elephant pens	12. drinking trough areas	15. public space

40 20 0 10

plan

39 The hand-hacked reinforced-concrete walls of the Elephant and Rhino Pavilion (BB92/6435).

lantern towers and the public entrances have boldly cantilevered timber canopies. In the paddocks, screen walls shield access to the drinking troughs and protect the keepers. The moat is used as an enclosure for agoutis (rodents of the guinea-pig family).

The irregular plan evolved as an unfettered expression of the requirements for space, temperature and light, as specified by zoologists. Circulation is directed around an S-plan public area, visitors moving from one animal pen to another in sequence with low-level viewing areas so that those who linger do not impede the flow. Light comes into the pens from the lanterns, while the public area is low and dark, with radiating laminated beams (24 ft/7·3 m in span) disposed in a tree-like manner to evoke a 'jungly' impression, an effect that has not been enhanced by the introduction of signs and banners.

Two groups of four pens in pairs, each pen served by a drinking trough, are supplemented by enclosed sick bays. Curved mosaic-tiled interior walls and doors with robust rounded concrete surrounds were intended to minimise damage by the animals and allow for

40 *(Right) The Elephant and Rhino Pavilion, eastern entrance (BB92/6434).*

41 *(Far right above) The interior of the Elephant and Rhino Pavilion in 1965 (Emap Architecture and the Casson Conder Partnership).*

42 *(Far right below) The interior of the Elephant and Rhino Pavilion in 1992 (BB92/6432).*

easy cleaning. To the west there is a washing pool and to the east there are staff rooms. Ditches with minimally obtrusive railings separate the public from the animals. A flue and an air intake rise through the centre of the building, partially disguised by timber columns.

The basement has heating and ventilation plant, food storage and preparation areas and wide passages for the clearance of quantities of dung, swept down into carts from ground-floor lobbies up to which food is hoisted.

Sources

BAL, RIBA Drawings, RAN 13 N/2.
Architect's Journal, 10 Jan 1962, p 58.
Architectural Review, July 1965, pp 13–20.
Architect and Building News, 14 July 1965, pp 69–74.
The Builder, 16 July 1965, pp 123–7.
Contract Journal, 26 Aug 1965.

Charles Clore Pavilion for Mammals   Plan 4:18

The Charles Clore Pavilion for Mammals [**43**, **44** and **45**] arose from the Zoo's 1958 redevelopment scheme. It provided one building for small mammals that had previously been housed in three places. Planning and research began in 1961 but building work had to await completion of the Elephant and Rhino Pavilion. The site is that of the 1868–9 Elephant and Rhinoceros House and its intended successor, the basement of which had been built to Tecton's designs in 1939.

The Clore Pavilion is architecturally unassuming with a plain, dark and uninformative exterior. The interior is similarly quiet, though more varied; features that would distract attention from the animals are avoided. There is 'aquarium principle' lighting on the ground floor and the basement contains the 'Moonlight World', where day and night are reversed by artificial lighting so that nocturnal animals can be viewed when active, the first large-scale exhibit of its kind and since widely copied elsewhere.

The building is formed of a group of low and irregularly massed blocks with unfenestrated brown stretcher-bond brick walls, splayed plinths and concrete roofs. A large glass north entrance porch, with underslung trussed steel masts, replaces a smaller glazed porch. Inside, dark-brown brick and paving is used throughout. There are

1965–7, following a £200,000 benefaction from Sir Charles Clore; brief by Desmond Morris, Curator of Mammals; Black, Bayes and Gibson (Kenneth Bayes and Maurice Green), architects; G E Wallis and Sons Limited, building contractors. Entrance porch replaced and basement fibreglass trees inserted 1990–1, J S Bonnington and Partners, architects.

43 (Left) The Charles Clore Pavilion for Mammals, east block interior from the west (BB92/6373).

44 (Above) The Charles Clore Pavilion for Mammals, showing 'aquarium principle' lighting to the cages in the west block, viewed from the east (BB92/6370).

subsidiary entrances and circulation is flexible along broad skylit passages, planted so as to resemble conservatories.

Inside there are 110 small cages lined with fibreglass rockwork, housing about as many mammal species. Sloping glass fronts prevent reflections and dirt kicked up by the animals from marring the view. The ground-floor cages are skylit and grouped in five distinct and varied areas to prevent monotony of viewing. In the west block they are set diagonally to the passage; another group is fronted by a water barrier for swimming mammals. There are open-air animal enclosures and, to the south east, a two-storey service block; the latter includes a kitchen whose large window allows the public to watch the animals' food being prepared. Few of the animals have access to the open air, but an air-conditioning system allows the keepers to vary the temperature from block to block to suit different animals. The cages are serviced by means of narrow passages equipped with breeding boxes.

Sources

The Builder, 20 Dec 1963, pp 1263–4.
Architect and Building News, 24 May 1967.
Building, 9 June 1967, pp 79–82.

45 The 'Moonlight World' exhibition of nocturnal animals in the Charles Clore Pavilion basement (BB92/6368).

46 *The Michael Sobell Pavilions for Apes and Monkeys, east block, showing tubular-steel space-frame roof (BB92/28113).*

Michael Sobell Pavilions
for Apes and Monkeys

Plan 4:40

The Michael Sobell Pavilions for Apes and Monkeys [**46** to **49**] replaced a Monkey House of 1926 – the successor to several earlier buildings – as well as Decimus Burton's 1820s terrace which led from the main gate. First plans were drawn up by Franz Stengelhofen in 1966, but these were abandoned as costly and unsuitable.

Architecturally the complex is functional and modest. Landscaped open-air enclosures dominate a design that aims for effacement in deference to the display of the animals. The latter is enhanced by a relationship between the indoor viewing dens and the open-air enclosures that allows the visitor to follow the movements of the animals. The principal feature of the fabric is the engineering of the tubular-steel space-frame roofs of the open-air enclosures. There are no public interiors, visitors being kept dry by covered walkways linking the pavilions.

Altogether there are five pavilions of various sizes. Each centres on a single-storey brown-brick section with chamfered angles and stepped plinths. Flat roofs of coffered reinforced concrete are latticed for continuous triangular skylights. The blocks contain fifteen indoor viewing dens and forty-four non-public inner cages in spacious service areas with overhead caging for the transfer of animals from one den to another. The indoor viewing dens have climbing frames, sloping floors to allow the outflow of urine and multi-pane glass fronts, low-silled so that small children do not have to be lifted. Despite this consideration the views are impaired by reflections.

1970–2, benefaction from Sir Michael Sobell; brief by Dr M R Brambell, Curator of Mammals; John Toovey and Jonathan Myles, architects; Anthony Hunt Associates, engineers; Trollope and Colls (City) Limited, building contractors.

Attached to the pavilion blocks are thirteen open-air enclosures, surrounded by wire mesh, with climbing frames and large branches. The animals are also able to climb and swing on the tubular-steel space-frame roofs (3ft 9in./1·14 m deep) in grids of 32 ft²/9·1 m². The framing has eighteen-face polyhedron joints known as Mero balls, a system devised by Max Meringhausen in Germany in 1940. The tensioned mesh has no intermediate supports and acts as a vertical trampoline.

The large south pavilion houses apes, the east pavilion larger monkeys, the north pavilion giant pandas and the two west pavilions small monkeys. The primates are able to move freely between indoors and outdoors through plastic flaps, and there are multiple

47 The Michael Sobell Pavilions, east block with walkway (BB92/6391).

access points to prevent the dominant animals from controlling the movements of the others.

Sources

Tubular Structures, March 1972, pp 2–8.

Zoological Society of London May 1972. *The Michael Sobell Pavilions for Apes and Monkeys*.

Toovey, J W and Brambell, M J 1976. 'The Michael Sobell Pavilions for Apes and Monkeys'. In *International Zoo Yearbook* XVI, pp 210–17.

Brambell, M J and Matthews, S J 1976. 'Primates and carnivores at Regent's Park'. In S Zuckerman (ed) *Zoological Society of London Symposium: 1826–1976 and Beyond*, pp 150–6.

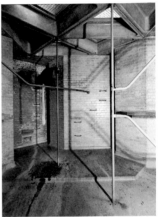

48 (*Below left*) *The Michael Sobell Pavilions, south block from the east* (BB92/28112).

49 (*Below*) *The Michael Sobell Pavilions, east block indoor viewing den* (BB92/28116).

50 The New Lion Terraces, lion enclosure from the north west (BB92/6343).

New Lion Terraces

Plan 4:60

1972–6, funding from Government and Sir Charles Clore; brief by Dr M R Brambell, Curator of Mammals; John Toovey, Colin Wears and Roger Balkwill, architects; Margaret Maxwell, landscape architect; R T James and Partners, engineers; J Jarvis and Sons Limited, building contractors; cost £666,232.

The New Lion Terraces [**50** to **54**] displaced Anthony Salvin junior's Lion House of 1875–7 [**8** and **Plan 2:15**] and the Cattle Sheds of 1869 which, from 1967, had included Chi-Chi's Giant Panda Enclosure. Considerable pride and satisfaction attached to the completion of this project; it came in the 150th anniversary year of the foundation of the Zoological Society of London and was the final component of the post-war reconstruction programme. The terraces are a rambling complex covering two acres of largely open space. The buildings are deliberately obscured in favour of landscaping that was intended as an improvement in the display and welfare of the animals, an approach that relied on the precedent of the lion and tiger exhibits at Whipsnade.

The completely irregular layout is divided into four distinct areas, three given over to large cats and the fourth to an aviary for water birds. The three cat areas provide outdoor enclosures for seven species and are served by four service blocks, one each for the lions and tigers and two shared by other species. These are small and discreet single-storey buildings with keepers' rooms and indoor sleeping and feeding dens – shuttered windows control visibility to the public. The service blocks have rendered brick walls and timber roofs on laminated beams. The windows in the complex are especially tough, consisting of a five-ply laminate of plastic and glass just under an inch (21 mm) thick. The dens are linked to the paddocks by caging incorporating crushes [**53**] for occasions when the animals need to be immobilised.

The outdoor areas comprise landscaped paddocks with ponds and moats of recirculated water. The planting, which extends right up to the public barriers, imitates habitats ranging from desert to jungle and the relief of the land is varied with rock-like concrete forms and basking platforms. The central viewing areas are separated from the animals by brick walls with inverted-arched windows, with low sills so as to allow children to see. Elsewhere the public stands behind railings and steel netting hung on steel tensile rods from screen walls of textured gunite concrete sprayed against lightweight formwork. Varied in height and profile, these walls are intended to resemble rock outcrops. They also serve to screen visitors from each other. At the approximate centre of the complex there is a concourse with steps leading to the covered walkways that link all four animal areas, analogous to those to be found at the Sobell Pavilions.

Sculpture enrichments include a finely lettered slate dedicatory plaque designed by Banks and Miles and cut by David Kindersley. Another stone inscribed 'THE LIONS HOUSE' was taken from above the entrance of the 1875–7 Lion House (the 'S' is a 1970s insertion). A large lion mask was similarly resited and there is a cast lion's head presented by its sculptor, William Timym, in 1976.

51 The New Lion Terraces, water birds' aviary from the west (BB92/6340)

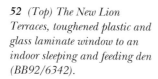

52 (Top) The New Lion Terraces, toughened plastic and glass laminate window to an indoor sleeping and feeding den (BB92/6342).

53 (Above right) The New Lion Terraces, caging and crush linking the lion enclosure to the indoor dens (BB92/6337).

54 (Above) The New Lion Terraces, lion mask resited from the Lion House of 1875–7 (BB91/28108).

Entrances to the complex are defined by cast-iron bollards, four to the west and four to the east. These are square-section pillars about 21 in. (55 cm) tall with lion-mask roundels above recessed panels with crossed bars, the panels open on the western group. Those to the west were reused from the Zoo's Main Gate and date from the 19th century, though one has been replaced. The east bollards are reused from the North Gate and appear to be 20th-century castings.

Sources

Zoological Society of London June 1976. *The New Lion Terraces.*
Architect's Journal, 16 June 1976, pp 1172–3.
Building, 14 Jan 1977, pp 79–86.
Brambell, M J and Matthews, S J 1976. 'Primates and carnivores at Regent's Park'. In S Zuckerman (ed) *Zoological Society of London Symposium: 1826–1976 and Beyond*, pp 154–6.

3

The Mappin Terraces and Aquarium

The Mappin Terraces (BB92/21613).

Mappin Terraces

Plan 4:33

1913–14, designed by Sir Peter Chalmers Mitchell; funded by John Newton Mappin; John James Joass, architect; Alexander Drew, engineer; D G Somerville and Company, reinforced-concrete contractors. Resurfaced and screens on steps remade 1968–72, John Toovey, architect. Vacated 1985. Listed Grade II.

55 *(Above) The Mappin Terraces from the east in about 1920 (RCHME, J J Samuels).*

The Mappin Terraces [**55** to **63**] are the Zoo's largest and most prominent feature. They were built as 'an installation for the panoramic display of wild animals' in the form of artificial mountains. This 'naturalistic' approach to animal display, which derived from the work of Carl Hagenbeck in Hamburg, was intended to improve living conditions for the animals and viewing conditions for the visitors.

The terraces are highly unconventional, in both constructional and architectural terms. Mitchell devised the basic arrangement, a three-tiered quadrant with hills, after being impressed by Continental panoramas, particularly one at Antwerp. Joass worked out the details and introduced Mappin, who did not live to see completion of the project. Joass claimed the inspiration of a classical hillside amphitheatre, but this invocation has the ring of retrospective rationalisation. In overseeing the project Joass would have been heavily dependent on the engineer, Alexander Drew, and the contractor, D G Somerville and Company. The latter firm was a practitioner (not licensee – no licence was needed) of the Kahn system, a method of concrete reinforcement invented by Julius Kahn in 1903 and widely used in car factories in Detroit by his brother Albert. Noted for the strength of its beams, this American system was used here in an ingenious and innovative way that was much praised at the time. The use of reinforced concrete was in

56 The Mappin Terraces from the east in 1990 (NBR 90/553).

large part dictated by London County Council building regulations. One result is that the internal structures hold a fascination which surpasses even that of the exteriors.

The Mappin Terraces have a quadrant plan with a radius of 288 ft (87 m). Concentric enclosures and terraces radiate and rise from the inner angle, the site of the Mappin Café (*see* below). There are three levels of animal enclosures, divided by terraces which function as public circulation paths, giving views both up and down. At the lowest level there is a pond (originally for waterfowl, later for penguins) and six paddocks (originally four), designed for deer and later used for other ruminants and pigs. The middle level has six bear enclosures and the upper level comprises four artificial mountains – 'goat hills' – rising to a height of about 70 ft (21 m). The terraces are linked by rebuilt stepped paths along the sides of the quadrant, with timber pergolas over the lower sections near the Mappin Café.

The lower deer paddocks are largely concrete surfaced. There are indoor shelters under the lower terrace and two small rock-faced blocks have been put up in the paddocks, perhaps as sties for pigs. The lower sides of the terrace paths originally had high walls pierced by openings, to obscure visitors from others below. These have been cut down to form railed dwarf walls.

The bear enclosures are fronted by a dry ditch, with spiky slate parapets added, and separated by rough-finished high walls of panelled brick and concrete. All opportunities for climbing were carefully excluded. The 'floors' are made of reinforced-concrete slabs

57 The Mappin Terraces, typical section showing the reinforced-concrete construction supporting the terraced enclosures as well as the interior of the Aquarium (based on sections published in The Times, *10 April 1914, and* The Builder, *22 May 1914, a survey plan by Gary Gabriel Associates, 1989, and RCHME site survey).*

1 *Deer Paddock;* 2 *Deer Shelter;*
3 *Lower Terrace;* 4 *Bear Enclosure;*
5 *Bear Tunnel;* 6 *Upper Terrace;*
7 *Sleeping Box;* 8 *Goat Hill;*
9 *High-Level Water Tank;*
10 *Aquarium Seawater Hall;*
11 *Exhibition Tank;*
12 *Service Passage;* 13 *Reservoir;*
14 *Filter Beds*

58 (Above) The Mappin Terraces, the contoured surfaces of the 'goat hills' (BB91/28081).

59 (Right) The Mappin Terraces, the underside of a bear enclosure (BB91/28082).

60 *The Mappin Terraces, reinforced-concrete framing supporting a 'goat hill' (BB92/6449).*

61 *The Mappin Terraces, a 'goat hill' interior showing a goat run (BB92/6448).*

between layers of wire mesh through which cement concrete was pushed to give an uneven finish. Cavities were formed for pools; the larger ones in the outer dens could originally be viewed through glass to see polar bears swimming. Under the upper terrace there are sleeping boxes for the bears, measuring about 6 ft (2 m) by 12 ft (4 m) and purposely small to be more cave-like.

The 'goat hills' step up irregularly to pronounced peaks whose surfaces are formed like those of the bear enclosure floors. Epoxy resurfacing accounts for colour variation, shading upwards from purple to yellow.

The outside walls of the quadrant are of pebbledashed concrete along the straight sides, with robustly hinged stable doors to hold the bears inside in the event of an escape. On the curved north-west face there are sheer drops from the 'goat hills'.

The 'goat hill' interiors are extraordinary spaces, each somewhat different. The contoured skins rest on elaborately latticed and trussed frames of crudely shuttered reinforced-concrete posts, beams and braces. Each interior is four to six bays long, each bay about 12 ft (4 m) long and 30 ft (9 m) across; the internal heights from the inserted floors are about 35 ft–40 ft (10 m–12 m). Below these floors the frames rest on columns within the Aquarium (*see* below). The members of the frame are about 9 in.–10 in.^{2} (25 cm^2), though in the west hill they are more substantial, about

62 The Mappin Terraces, a 'goat hill' interior with water tank on floor (BB92/6447).

14 in.–15 in.^{2} (36 cm^2), because intermediate columns were omitted at the lower level to allow for an open hall measuring 42 ft (12·7 m) across (the Aquarium's Seawater Hall).

Within the frames there are massive steel water tanks serving the Aquarium; from the outset one such tank served the bears' ponds. The north-west hill has the floor of two bays given over to a water tank. Doors give out on to the lower slopes of the hills for the distribution of hay and feed, the openings positioned so as to encourage the goats to come into public view. There are high-level louvred vents for air discharged from the Aquarium. Concrete-framed goat runs lead from under the lower terrace to the hills, while bear tunnels link the bear enclosures with their ditches. The areas under the bear enclosures and the terraces consist of low service spaces with numerous posts. A passage gives access to the rear of the bears' sleeping boxes.

Sources

English Heritage (London Region), Historians' File.
BAL, RIBA Drawings, RAN 30 J/5.
Building News, 26 Sept 1913, pp 436–8.
The Builder, 22 May 1914, pp 617–21.
Concrete and Constructional Engineering, 1914, pp 21–30.
The Times, 10 April 1914.

63 The Mappin Terraces, a 'goat hill' interior (BB92/6445).

Mappin Café

Plan 4:34

1914–20, funded by John Newton Mappin; John James Joass, architect. Closed 1985. Listed Grade II.

The Mappin Café is at the lower (south) angle of the Mappin Terraces, a small quadrant within the larger quadrant [**64** and **65**]. This 'tea pavilion', in Italian Renaissance style, was part of the 1913 scheme but, at Mappin's request, it was left 'until the best possible provision has been made for the animals'. Work began just before the outbreak of World War I, but was postponed for six years before being completed to modified plans.

The Café is a single-storey red-brick building with stone dressings and pantiled roofs, characterised by paired Tuscan columns, French windows, bracketed eaves and pavilion towers at the three angles. Its curved façade has a long open colonnade on to a terrace from which the Mappin Terraces can be viewed. The building was entered from this terrace as well as via steps on the south-eastern side. The interior has simple classical mouldings and there were serving areas along the straight sides.

Sources
BAL, RIBA Drawings, RAN 30 J/4.
Building News, 26 Sept 1913, p 437.

Aquarium   Plan 4:33

The Aquarium [**57** and **66** to **71**] is housed under the Mappin Terraces. The space had been set aside for an aquarium from 1913 when the Terraces were laid out, but detailed planning was deferred by war until 1921–2. Briefs were provided following visits to aquariums in Amsterdam, Antwerp, Brussels, Berlin and Dresden. The spacious tank-lined public interiors are very dark, the fish being made prominent by artificial light filtering through the tanks to the viewer. The water, including natural seawater, circulates through an elaborate closed system. The cost of the building made a separate admission charge necessary for many years.

The Aquarium originally had stripped classical external elevations at the east and west angles of the Mappin Terraces – rendered brick with blind arches, oculi and pilaster strips. These have all but disappeared. The eastern façades have been refaced with Poilite asbestos-cement fixed as weatherboarding. A single-storey flat-roofed range projects from the curved north side of the Mappin Terraces to house the north passage. This and the west end elevation have been refaced in stock brick.

The Aquarium has freshwater, seawater and tropical halls running in a curvilinear sequence for about 450 ft (136 m). The halls consist of broad circulation areas with perimeter tanks. The lower part of the 'goat hill' structural frame is evident in a row of massive reinforced-concrete piers. The Seawater Hall is open across the full width. Since the interiors are so dark, they are architecturally plain, 'domesticated' only by coved cornices. In the Seawater Hall there is an abstract glass fish sculpture made and donated by Catherine Yass in 1986.

1923–4, brief by E G Boulenger, Curator of Reptiles; John James Joass, architect; Alexander Gibb and Partners, engineers; J Jarvis and Sons Limited, building contractors; Joan Beauchamp Procter, rockwork design; cost around £55,000. Refaced to west 1951, and to east 1965, Franz Stengelhofen, architect. Listed Grade II.

64 (Far left above) The Mappin Café, built 1914–20, John James Joass, architect, from the south east (BB92/20477).

65 (Far left below) The tea-terrace colonnade of the Mappin Café (BB92/21611).

66 (Below) The entrance to the Aquarium in 1924 (RCHME, Bedford Lemere).

67 (Right) The entrance to the Aquarium in 1992 (BB92/28087).

68 (Below) A cut-away perspective view of the Aquarium (from a painting in the Aquarium entrance lobby).

Altogether there are more than 100 exhibition tanks up to 30 ft (9 m) wide (sea turtles inhabiting the largest) with glass fronts up to 1¼ in. (32 mm) thick. The walls of the tanks were originally of slate, but these have largely been replaced with reinforced waterproof cement. Near the east entrance there are offices and research laboratories. Service passages run behind the tanks at a level higher than the public floors, to give keepers ready access to the tops of the tanks.

Fish need stable temperatures, saline balance (if in seawater) and aerated and circulating water. The Aquarium's electrically powered closed system of water circulation accommodates vast amounts of fresh and sea water, natural seawater circulating in use for many years, topped up annually by supplies brought by road

69 (Left) The Aquarium, the Freshwater Hall from the east (BB92/20478).

70 (Below) The Aquarium, the Seawater Hall from the east (BB92/28088).

71 *The Aquarium, north service passage from the east (BB92/6438).*

tanker. The system comprises reservoirs under the public floors and at the level of the service corridors, with filter beds, ventilating plant, store rooms and an engine room under parts of the bear dens, as well as high-level tanks in the 'goat hills'. Water is pumped up from the underground tank to the high-level tanks then allowed to fall to the exhibition tanks, from where it travels to the filter beds before running back to the underground reservoir. Various temperatures are maintained through separate circulation systems to suit different species.

Sources

BAL, RIBA Drawings, RAN 30 K/1, SOS D/1.
The Builder, 13 April 1923, p 608; 24 Sept 1965.
Vevers, H G 1976. 'Management of a public aquarium'. In S Zuckerman (ed) *Zoological Society of London Symposium: 1826–1976 and Beyond*, pp 111–15.

4

Aviaries

*The Northern (Snowdon) Aviary
(BB92/21618).*

AVIARY

Raven's Cage

Plan 4:43

1829, Decimus Burton, architect. 'Renovated' 1927. 'Reconstructed' 1948 following war damage. Moved 1971. Listed Grade II.

72 *(Above) The Raven's Cage in 1832 (from C F Partington,* National History and Views of London, *1832, drawn by T H Shepherd, engraved by J Shury).*

73 *(Above right) The Raven's Cage, as reconstructed in 1948 and 1971 (BB92/20474).*

The former Raven's Cage [**72** and **73**] is a rebuilding of an aviary put up as summer caging for macaws. It originally stood just north west of the Clock Tower. No longer used as an aviary, it survives simply as a decorative and commemorative object.

It is unlikely that any of the cage's 19th-century fabric remains, though early views confirm that the cage's appearance is essentially as built. It is no more than a large birdcage of the sort that might have formed part of any early menagerie.

The octagonal cage stands on a brick plinth made in 1971. It has a wire-mesh covered cast and wrought-iron frame of square-section members with arches to each face and a tented head with a moulded finial.

By the 1840s the cage had been converted to accommodate a vulture and a small house had been added on the north-western side; this was removed, probably in 1948.

Sources
The Mirror, 29 Sept 1832, p 281.

African Aviary

Plan 4:41

The African (formerly Eastern) Aviary [**74**, **75** and **76**] replaced an aviary of 1827–8 by Decimus Burton on the same site. The Victorian building, now largely remodelled, was claimed as the best of its type in the country when it opened. It was vastly superior to standard cage-aviaries and was more closely comparable to the Zoo's animal houses. To protect vulnerable birds there was a hot-water heated interior with indoor cages viewable from a public passage. The floors of these cages were set close to eye level to make the birds more readily visible. Originally, there were ten outdoor cages on the south side, the two largest at either end.

The partially surviving 19th-century brick block retains its original white-brick end walls under stuccoed pedimental gables. There are pilaster strips and finely gauged brick arches. The smaller south arches housed the doors to the public passage; the larger

1863–4, Anthony Salvin junior, architect; Lucas Brothers, builders, cost £2,688. Remodelled with new outdoor caging and renamed 1989–90, brief from Peter Olney, Curator of Birds; John S Bonnington Partnership, architects; Whitby and Bird, structural engineers; landscaping by Derek Howarth and Ron Whittle, filmset experts; cost £485,000.

74 *The African Aviary, showing the steel footing that holds the wires of the outdoor caging (BB92/6304).*

75 (Above) The African Aviary, tensioned wires and imitation African habitat (BB92/6310).

76 (Above right) The African Aviary, detail of a steel 'fan' (BB92/6309).

arches must have lit the indoor cages. Other traces of the passage and the front slope of the roof were removed during the enlargement of the outdoor cages. The remaining indoor parts of the building have been converted and skylit as shelters and holding cages. A hipped-roofed rear block to the north east has probably always been used for services and keepers' accommodation.

The outdoor caging is a contiguous but wholly separate structure that is much larger than the earlier caging, to give eagles, hawks and vultures more space and the public better views. To this end the caging within the frame was designed to be virtually invisible in what is claimed to be the first wire aviary built in Britain. Imitation African habitats comprise another important feature of the design.

The caging has a tall hooped tubular-steel frame with parallel wires stretched across the arches of the upper part of the frame and anchored at either end to fans on wing-like steel footings with massive concrete foundations. The 0·9 mm diameter wires (there are 1,688 in total) run for a length of about 100 ft (30 m) at 1·2 in. (31 mm) intervals as well as vertically in front of the lower parts of the frames. They are made of a strong stainless-steel alloy developed for North Sea oil structures. Within the four cages there are artificial trees, rockwork, ponds and a waterfall.

Sources
Information kindly supplied by the John S Bonnington Partnership.

Peafowl Aviary   Plan 4:76

The Peafowl Aviary of 1903 adjoins the north-west corner of the Bird House. It is a simple row of bird runs, a building type established in an agricultural context as hen-runs and pheasantries. It originally comprised wooden shelters behind wire-mesh covered runs. The shelters have been rebuilt in concrete blocks and corrugated-sheet roofing. The ten-bay steel frame over the runs, measuring about 108 ft (33 m) by 23 ft (7 m), has arched-head trusses with I and T-section members and wrought-iron tie and king rods.

Southern Aviary   Plan 4:35

The Southern Aviary of 1905 [82] is the largest of the Zoo's early aviaries. It is a simple, light metal-framed structure of the type that is general for aviaries, but impressive for its size. It was an early attempt to provide a natural environment for birds, giving them space for free flight.

Measuring about 130 ft (40 m) by 60 ft (18 m), it rises to a height of approximately 33 ft (10 m). Wire mesh covers a thirteen-bay tubular-metal frame stabilised by central uprights and braces, and external buttresses. The landscaping of artificial rockwork and ponds, with mature willows, was a reordering of what had been the Southern Ponds from about 1860.

Owls' Aviary   Plan 4:5

The Owls' Aviary of 1905 is another pheasantry-like structure with caging arranged as if with a 'palace front', that is with a wide arch-fronted central bay and slightly taller paired outer bays that formerly had gabled heads.

The 100 ft (30 m) row consists of fifteen open cages in front of simple shelter huts, probably of timber originally but rebuilt in concrete blocks. The wire-mesh cages have light tubular-metal framing on a brick plinth.

North Pheasantry

Plan 4:4

About 1900. Resited further north 1906–7. More than doubled in length to the west 1913–14. Additions cleared in 1960s.

The North Pheasantry, as it survives, dates from 1906–7. Its caging has parallel vaults arranged 4:2:6; the broader middle pair was originally central, the two westernmost bays of the 1906–7 building having been demolished.

The shelter sheds to the rear are of stock brick with ornamental dentillation and a lean-to roof. The wire-mesh covered, light tubular-metal framing covers an area about 128 ft (39 m) by 16 ft (5 m). The frame stands on a plinth and is divided into twelve shallow-arched roofs, each trussed with tie and king rods.

Owl and Parrot Aviaries

Plan 4:8 and 4:55

1957, Franz Stengelhofen, architect.

The Owl Aviary north of the East Footbridge [**Plan 4:8**] and the Parrot Aviary north east of the Parrot House [**Plan 4:55**] were both built as parts of public toilet blocks. They are simple buildings, roughly rectangular with stock-brick walls and flat roofs. Caging around the exteriors consists of light tubular-steel framing and wire mesh in front of mosaic walling.

Gibbon Cage and Cockatoo Aviary

Plan 4:47 and 4:48

1960–2, Franz Stengelhofen, architect. Pool bases land-scaped 1981.

The Gibbon Cage (treated here as if it were an aviary because of its physical form) [**Plan 4:47**] and the Cockatoo Aviary [**Plan 4:48**] are similar structures, respectively about 100 ft (30 m) and 66 ft (20 m) long (twelve and eight bays), each about 16 ft (5 m) wide and 25 ft (8 m) tall. Wire mesh covers square-section and tubular-steel framing that rises up with inward sloping sides to a squared head. Originally these cages stood in pools of water, intended primarily to keep the gibbons off the ground.

The Gibbon Cage has springy trapeze bars to provide the gibbons with the opportunity to exercise by arm-swinging the length of the cage. When built this was the longest artificial gibbon run in the world.

South Pheasantry

Plan 4:71

1962, Franz Stengelhofen, architect.

The South Pheasantry comprises two ranges of cages to the south west of the Bird House. A group of eight cages (about 78 ft/24 m long) runs north–south and, to its east, a group of five cages (about 60 ft/18 m long) runs east–west. They comprise timber shelter sheds under lean-to roofs and light tubular-steel frame caging with some shallow-arched heads.

Northern (Snowdon) Aviary

Plan 4:2

The Northern Aviary, widely known as the Snowdon Aviary [**77** to **81**], is the largest and by far the most spectacular of the Zoo's aviaries. It is as expressionistically birdlike in its lightness as the contemporary Elephant and Rhino Pavilion is elephantine in its bulk. The building was pioneering in two key respects – it is a large tension structure and it is made of aluminium. An early example of a walk-through aviary, its landscaping is integrated with the circulation system to allow the public close-up views of birds in a wide variety of habitats.

The aviary arose from Sir Hugh Casson's 1958 Development Plan as a replacement for the Great Aviary of 1888, situated near the Main Gate. Anthony Armstrong-Jones (Lord Snowdon) was commissioned to design the building in 1960 on the strength of his design for a birdcage at Mereworth Castle and a recommendation by the Duke of Edinburgh, then President of the Zoological Society and Lord Snowdon's brother-in-law. Armstrong-Jones had trained (but not qualified) in architecture so Casson brought in Cedric Price, who was soon joined by his friend Frank Newby.

The Zoo asked for a walk-through aviary on an awkward site: the steeply sloping north bank of the Regent's Canal. It was to be

1962–4, with a benefaction of £50,000 from Jack Cotton; Anthony Armstrong-Jones (Lord Snowdon) and Cedric Price, architects; Frank Newby (of F J Samuely and Partners), engineer; Leonard Fairclough (London) Limited, general contractor; Carter Horsley, suppliers of superstructure; Westminster Engineering, suppliers of mesh cladding; Margaret Maxwell (of Bridgwater, Shepheard and Epstein), landscape consultant; cost £125,000 (about half superstructure, half landscaping).

78 The Northern (Snowdon)
Aviary from the south
(BB92/6284).

77 (Previous page) The
skeletal form of the Northern
(Snowdon) Aviary (Alti-
Cam/David M Kay).

an eye-catching structure enclosing the maximum space with good views from both outside and within. Models and computers were used to develop the innovative design. Technical difficulties delayed the opening until 1965.

The aviary is large and measures about 150 ft (45 m) by 63 ft (19 m), with a maximum height of 80 ft (24 m). Like most other aviaries it comprises a frame and mesh cladding. The lightweight aluminium frame is made up of tubular components linked by steel cables. It fixes on opposed pairs of sheer legs (54 ft/16 m long), anchored on massive concrete footings and angled outwards at about 60°. The sheer legs are made up of multiple curved extrusions welded together into 24 in. (61 cm) diameter tubes with conical bases and heads. The structure is filled out and held in tension by four tetrahedral frames flanking the sheer legs in pairs of unequal sizes (55 ft/17 m and 43 ft/13 m tall) with 12 in. (30 cm) diameter tubes joined by specially cast angle pieces. Held in position only by cables, these tetrahedrons give the impression of floating in space. The tensioned steel-rope cables (between 1 in./2·5 cm and 2 1/2 in./6·5 cm in diameter) are plastic sheathed

76

and U-bolted, with central steel rings. The mesh cladding is of black anodised welded aluminium netting in 12 ft (3·6 m) by 4 ft (1·2 m) panels. The mesh is open enough to allow sparrows in; were it not it would solidify in icy and snowy conditions.

Public circulation is along the main axis. Steps lead up to curtained doorways at either end. The internal walkway follows a zigzag path with its centre section a cantilevered pre-stressed reinforced-concrete 'bridge', angled sharply into space, up and away from the canal bank. The railings have aluminium handrails, with timber slats added for safety.

The canal bank, cut away and terraced with a reinforced-concrete retaining wall, is disguised as a cliff with nesting holes. There is an internal water system with a fast-flowing east waterfall over faceted concrete and a slower west waterfall stepped over basins, which form small ponds for water birds. There is a larger pool at ground level.

79 The Northern (Snowdon) Aviary, showing the internal walkway (BB92/6285).

80 (Right) The Northern (Snowdon) Aviary, showing the canal-bank retaining wall with nesting holes (BB92/6279).

81 (Below) The Northern (Snowdon) Aviary, detail of frame on east side (BB92/6283).

The system is operated by a recirculating pump in a plant-room under the east waterfall. The interior is designed to be viewed from paths immediately north and south of the structure as well as from the walkway.

Sources

English Heritage (London Region), Historians' File.
Architect's Journal, 27 April 1961, p 599.
Architectural Review, Dec 1961, pp 417–18 and Sept 1965, p 185.
The Builder, 4 June 1965, p 1231.
Building Design, 4 Oct 1991, pp 34–5.

5

Ponds, Pools and Enclosures

*Three Island Pond
(BB92/6376).*

Three Island Pond Plan 4:57

1832, Decimus Burton, architect. Enlarged 1852. Altered 1961 and 1976.

Three Island Pond is an irregularly shaped artificial pond of about 130 ft (40 m) by 165 ft (50 m) in extent, the south side of which has been incorporated into the New Lion Terraces. There are concrete linings to the water areas and an outer moat. The enclosure is inhabited by pelicans, coots and ducks and the three islands are planted with large willows and other trees.

Former Prairie Dog Enclosure

To the north of Three Island Pond there is an irregularly shaped grassed enclosure. Formed in 1905 for the display of squirrels, but soon given over to prairie dogs, it is about 55 ft (17 m) across with dwarf perimeter walling of coped reconstituted stone. Latterly a small budgerigar aviary stood on the site before it was again used for squirrels and then abandoned.

Sea Lion Pond and Viewing Stand Plan 4:38

1905. Viewing stand, dens and kiosk added 1967, Franz Stengelhofen, architect. Kiosk awning added 1989–90. Pond remade 1992.

The Sea Lion Pond [82], formed for sea lions (fur seals) and penguins, was London Zoo's first attempt at naturalistic, or Hagenbeckian, outdoor display and was based on similar structures in Paris and Cologne. Its design, in principle if not in detail, may be due to Sir Peter Chalmers Mitchell, the Zoo's principal exponent of this type of naturalism.

The irregular pond, about 100 ft (30 m) long, is concrete-lined with grassed and railed banks. Small islands have been removed in remaking the pond. At the west end there is a 12 ft (4 m) high rockwork screen made up of limestone, sandstone, slate and concrete. Originally this was much taller, rising to a height of about 30 ft (9 m) to resemble a cliff-face. It disguises sleeping dens and a service room. The bank in front of the dens serves as a diving platform.

On the south side of the pond is a reinforced-concrete addition that serves as a stand for watching the feeding of the sea lions, with animal dens and paddocks to the south, and a terrace over a kiosk to the east.

The steps of the viewing stand are sheltered by a cantilevered roof with segmental vaults on six pairs of square-section uprights. The back of the stand is enclosed by a black-brick screen. Below there are three dens, formerly used to accommodate dogs, with wire-mesh enclosed paddocks. To the east, seven columns support the terrace which has a shuttered-concrete and railed parapet over the brick-faced kiosk. Three tensile roofs on tubular-steel framing form awnings in front of the kiosk.

Sources
Pall Mall Gazette, 17 Jan 1905.
The Daily Telegraph, 12 April 1905.

82 The Sea Lion Pond in 1991, prior to the removal of the islands during relandscaping (BB91/28071).

Prairie Marmot Enclosure

The Prairie Marmot Enclosure was formed as a Coypu Pond and built with the Insect House [**Plan 4:15**] (*see* above) to the north. At the time of its construction it was a novel display because it was free of bars or fencing.

It is a rectangular area about 33 ft (10 m) by 12 ft (4 m) within a retaining wall with quadrant angles. This wall has a rounded stone capping, part replaced in concrete, undercut so that the coypus could not climb out. Rockwork at the centre conceals sleeping boxes. Water around the rockwork has been drained and an enclosing fence erected.

1912–13, with funding from Sir James K Caird. Relandscaped 1983.

81

Reptiliary

Plan 4:19

1922. Remade 1971, John Toovey, architect; plaque designed by Banks and Miles, cut by David Kindersley. Converted 1992.

The Reptiliary was originally an Otter Pond, the forming of which followed on from the opening of the adjacent West Tunnel in 1920. The otters were rehoused in 1969 and the pond was refitted for two black beavers donated to the Queen by the Hudson's Bay Company and passed on to the Zoo in 1970. Subsequently the enclosure was converted for iguanas.

The enclosure was originally simply a square pond with a central island. It was remade as a sunken enclosure with a deep water area, rockwork and shrub landscaping. Low stock-brick perimeter walling with glass panels dates from this conversion. To adapt the enclosure for lizards the water area was backfilled and the rockwork relandscaped.

Mongoose Enclosure

Plan 4:64

83 The Penguin Pool, built 1934, Tecton, architects (BB92/21609).

The small open enclosure south east of the Elephant and Rhino Pavilion was built in 1922 as a racoon enclosure and used for red pandas before passing to mongooses. It consists of a grassy mound within a reinforced-concrete octagonal retaining wall. This wall has an inwardly splayed upper lip to prevent escape. An ailanthus tree at the centre of the mound was uprooted in the destructive storm of October 1987.

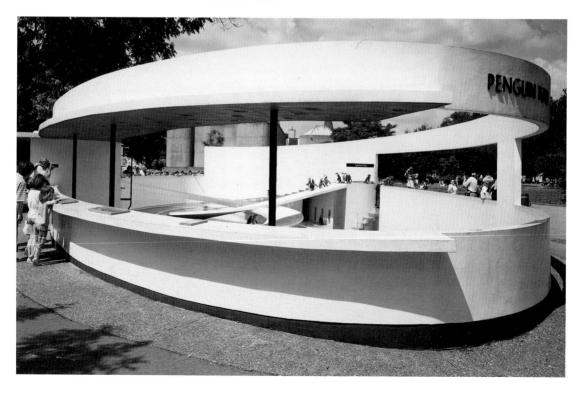

Penguin Pool

Plan 4:62

The Penguin Pool [**83** to **86**], probably the best known of all the Zoo's buildings, was built on a site previously goose paddocks. The commission for its design went to Tecton and followed the enthusiastic reception given to their revolutionary Gorilla House (*see above*). Lubetkin was given liberty to design an exhibition piece, a pointedly non-naturalistic stage for the antics of the penguins that avoids any appearance of caging. The 'Constructivist' design is an influential and popular piece of early modernist architecture. The structure was also a notable demonstration of the potential of reinforced concrete.

The pool has a neatly self-contained elliptical plan (about 36 ft/11 m by 118 ft/36 m). Made of reinforced concrete throughout, the material was most innovatively used in the interlocking ramps at the centre, each about 46 ft (14 m) long and 4 ft (1·2 m) wide with thicknesses varying from 3 in. to 6 in. (8 cm to 15 cm). These ramps are cantilevered without intermediate support – a construction that was only possible by virtue of exemption from London County Council building regulations.

To the north there are nesting boxes over which slate steps rise to the head of one ramp. There is an external pit for cleaning and supervising the nesting boxes. To the south the other ramp leads the birds to a diving tank, with a plate-glass front at public eye-level. This has an adjoining top-lit canopy, for shade and architectural balance. The poolside ambulatory is made of slate-slab paving

1934, brief by Sir Peter Chalmers Mitchell, Secretary, Dr Geoffrey Marr Vevers, Superintendent, and David Seth-Smith, Curator of Birds and Mammals; Tecton (Berthold Lubetkin and Lindsey Drake), architects; J L Kier and Company (with Ove Arup and Felix Samuely as structural engineers), general contractors; cost about £2,000. Refurbished 1985–7, Avanti Architects (John Allan), with Berthold Lubetkin and Arup Associates; cost about £280,000, with grants from English Heritage and Peter Palumbo. Listed Grade I.

84 The Penguin Pool, showing mosaic-lined pond, steps and interlocking ramps (BB92/21608).

covered with plastic rubber (cork chippings, rubber and *ciment fondu*). The perimeter wall is monolithic, though broken to allow public viewing. It acts as a retaining wall for the pool and as a sounding board for the penguins' calls.

Refurbishment consisted of reinstating missing details and renewing the concrete finishes, the mosaic lining and the colour scheme. The latter formed an important part of the design: white walls, with blue for the mosaic-lined pond, grey for the steps and red for the ambulatory.

85 (Right) The Penguin Pool, showing nesting boxes and cantilevered interlocking ramps (BB92/21610).

86 (Below) The Penguin Pool (based on a plan published in Architect and Building News, *1 June 1934, and site survey – original drawing in BAL, RIBA Drawings Collection, RAN 19 D/2). 1 Diving Tank; 2 Steps with Nesting Boxes below; 3 External Pit*

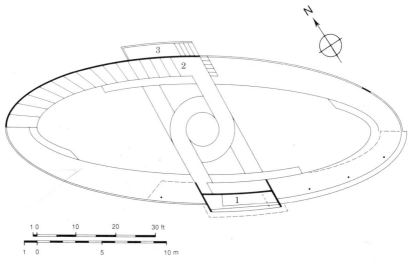

Despite Tecton's sincere attempt to consider the needs of the animals, the Penguin Pool has been criticised as unsuited to its purpose, although the birds are said to breed successfully.

Sources

BAL, RIBA Drawings, RAN 19 D/2, RAN 30 L/2[1].

Architect's Journal, 14 June 1934, pp 856–9, 873–4; 25 Nov 1987, p 7; 5 Feb 1992, pp 28–37.

Architect and Building News, 1 June 1934, pp 254–5.

Architectural Review, July 1934, pp 17–19.

Allan, J 1992. *Berthold Lubetkin: Architecture and the Tradition of Progress*, pp 208–12.

Coe, P and Reading, M 1981. *Lubetkin and Tecton: Architecture and Social Commitment*, pp 126–7.

Cormorant Pond   Plan 4:63

The Cormorant Pond [87] was formed as a Panda Pit, then converted to a Seal Pond, before being used for cormorants. It is a circular concrete-lined pond of about 43 ft (13 m) diameter. At its centre is a rock-strewn concrete island. To the north east is a disused den with steps down for service access. The low perimeter wall is formed of red, rough-faced, composition stone blocks. The conversion presumably involved relining for filling with water.

About 1950. Converted 1959–60, Franz Stengelhofen, architect.

87 The Cormorant Pond viewed from the south west (BB91/28075).

Penguin Incubation Centre

Plan 4:65

About 1960. Reconstructed 1971.

This enclosure immediately north west of the Children's Zoo was formed as a small Seal Pond. Its back areas were reconstructed to accommodate capybaras (large Brazilian rodents), but occupancy has since passed to penguins. It has an irregular ovoid plan with a concrete-lined crescent of water in front of rockwork and a painted brick rear wall. A concrete dwarf wall and shrubs separate the pond from the public.

Children's Zoo and Farm

Plan 4:66–69

Founded 1938, incorporating deer shed of about 1920. Western stables, 1959; Nocturnal House, 1963; Milking Parlour, 1963 as Chimp Den, converted 1973–5, with addition of stable sheds and enclosing wall; Animal Handling Building 1967; eastern farm pens, about 1938, rebuilt 1967, paddock layout altered 1977, dens inserted 1983. All by Zoological Society of London architects.

The Children's Zoo is set off from the rest of the Zoo as an area where children, particularly those of an urban upbringing, can come into close contact with animals, generally those that are either young or domesticated. In its early years most of the site remained open. To the west a small deer shed, with timber-log walls and a roof of fishscale tiles, was incorporated and, to the east, a range of pens was erected.

Scattered across the Children's Zoo is a miscellany of small buildings dating from the period 1959 to 1975, when the Zoo as a whole was undergoing redevelopment. To the west a range of stables [**Plan 4:66**] with ten stalls accommodates goats, ponies and wallabies. It is a simple brick and timber structure with a lean-to roof. To the east is the Nocturnal House, a flat-roofed unfenestrated block kept dark to allow children to see nocturnal animals awake.

Further east stands the Milking Parlour [**Plan 4:68**]. This was erected as the latter-day venue for the Chimps' Tea Party, an event of renown staged at London Zoo from 1926 to 1972. This painted-brick block has a monopitch roof extending eastwards to cover a forecourt or stage beyond which rise steps with seating. A cow shed to the west links to a stabling range converted to offices.

The Animal Handling Building [**88** and **Plan 4:67**] comprises a flat roof on square-section steel supports over an area informally divided by low brick walls, with a central duck pond open to the sky. The walls guide visitors around a series of spaces where rabbits and other animals are made accessible on 'touch-shelves'.

The rebuilt farm pens, for sheep and pigs, stand to the east [**Plan 4:69**] and have timber lean-to roofs over concrete-block dens. The curved paddock railings are reused public barriers from around one of the outdoor cages of the 1875–7 Lion House. The east wall behind the pens is decorated with a mural depicting a farm scene.

Wolf Wood

Plan 4:75

1963, Franz Stengelhofen and Colin Wears, architects.

Wolf Wood is an area of fenced parkland backing on to the Broad Walk. The land was brought into the Zoo in 1935, intended for the Children's Zoo. As laid out there are two enclosures based on a comparable Wolf

Wood at Whipsnade. The only structures are bunker-like concrete and brick lairs. One of these is flanked by screens of timber posts.

Flamingo Pool

Plan 4:54

The Flamingo Pool was formed on the site of a wolverine, jackal and fox enclosure. Latterly used by pelicans it has now reverted to its original use, with a smaller water area and grassed banks. There is an irregular concrete-lined pond and a low service building.

88 (Below) The Animal Handling Building in the Children's Zoo (BB92/21607).

1965. Relandscaped 1992 with funding from BOC Limited.

Otter Pool

Plan 4:16

1969, brief by Jeremy Harris, otter expert; John Toovey, architect; stoneware plaque designed by Banks and Miles.

89 *(Above) The Otter Pool viewed from the north (BB92/6363).*

The Otter Pool [**89**] was built on the site of an earlier Beaver Pond. The enclosure has, as its central feature, a raised pool retained by a concrete wall pierced by glass panels to allow visitors to see the otters underwater. Within the pool there is a ramp. There are steps up to the pool from the surrounding sunken area which is planted with trees and enclosed by low stock-brick walling on top of which a railing has been added to comply with the 1988 Zoo Licensing Act. To the north there is a small brick-walled den.

6

Gates, Tunnels and Bridges

*The West Footbridge of 1960–1
(BB92/6414).*

Main Gate

Plan 4:32

*1928, brief by Sir Peter
Chalmers Mitchell and Joan
Beauchamp Procter; Sir
Edward Guy Dawber, archi-
tect; columns made by G E
Wallis and Sons Limited.
South-west kiosk added and
south terrace laid out 1971
with the Sobell Pavilions,
John Toovey, architect.
Terrace layout altered 1984
and 1988.*

90 *(Above) The Main Gate from
the west showing the unusual
columns of the loggia, flanked by
pavilions (BB92/6360).*

The Main Gate [**90**] replaced a narrower gate set between twin
lodges. It is in the Italianate style that John James Joass had introduced to the Zoo, with 'just a hint of the fabulous' in its columns.
A semicircular court within the gate was originally enclosed by a
colonnade of similar design, its purpose to fan visitors out across
the gardens.

The gate comprises two pavilions flanking a loggia. The pavilions are built of Crowborough brick with large incised stucco panels, keyed oculi and pyramidal tiled roofs with bracketed eaves.
They house ticket offices, with a tank room above on one side. The
loggia, which originally sheltered ticket kiosks, has coupled and
distinctively moulded artificial stone columns. Public toilet blocks
formerly flanked the pavilions and the area south west of the
colonnade was laid out as a reptile rock garden.

The entrance court within the gate has been wholly reordered.
The colonnade was cleared (traces survive on the inner faces of the
pavilions), then a brick and concrete kiosk, latterly a shop, was
built to the south west of the west pavilion and a terrace was laid
out displacing the reptile garden. The Main Gate became the
Zoo's only public entrance and the layout was again altered with
the addition of a steel space-deck canopy and small kiosks on the
south side of the terrace. Circulation was revised again with new
ticket kiosks on the terrace and enclosing timber trellis pergolas
and fencing.

On the outer side of the Main Gate there is an iron pergola which appears to be part of the 1928 layout. It incorporates slender Corinthian cast-iron columns that may have been resited at that time.

Sources

BAL, RIBA Drawings, RAN 30 K/5[1–2].
Architect's Journal, 12 Dec 1928, pp 837–8.

North Gate (Bird Incubation and Rearing Centre) Plan 4:6 and 7

The group of buildings that forms the Bird Incubation and Rearing Centre was formerly the Zoo's North Gate. It has three sections: the former North Gate itself, flanked by a former toilet block and the former North Gate Kiosk.

The North Gate [**91** and **Plan 4:6**] was formed as an open-sided six-bay range sheltering ticket kiosks and turnstiles. It was a very similar building to the Discovery Centre (*see* below). It has timber posts with brackets and shaped eaves brackets to a hipped tiled roof. Block partitions and caging have been inserted and a timber lean-to extends to the north where the remains of an iron pergola survive. The former public toilet block to the west has painted brick walls and a hipped tiled roof.

1926, probably by Walter, Hearn and Chuter, architects. North Gate Kiosk added 1936, Tecton (Berthold Lubetkin), architects. Closed and altered for use as a store, 1975. Converted 1989–90, Colin Wears with the John S Bonnington Partnership, architects. North Gate Kiosk Listed Grade II.

91 *The North Gate viewed from the east (BB92/6325).*

92 The North Gate Kiosk with Lubetkin's distinctive canopy in 1937 (RCHME, H Felton).

The North Gate Kiosk of 1936 [**92** and **Plan 4:7**], added on the east side of the North Gate, was based on Lubetkin's 1934 Shelter and Kiosk for Whipsnade and was paralleled by his Main Entrance at Dudley Zoo of 1936–7. All three use curved canopies as bold architectural flourishes.

The kiosk included a gatekeeper's lodge to the west, roofed as part of the North Gate, and, beyond a passage to the exit turnstiles, a block for a cloakroom and refreshment bar. This is a flat-roofed dark-red brick range with windows in projecting concrete surrounds. The canopy to the south comprises a continuous slab of reinforced-concrete (6 in./15 cm thick) in a sinusoidal wave on slender (3 1/2 in./9 cm diameter) cylindrical steel columns at 15 ft (4·5 m) intervals. Towards the east end the columns are set back to accommodate a faience-tiled serving counter, now removed.

The exit between the former gatekeeper's lodge and cloakroom is via a pair of turnstiles in reinforced-concrete surrounds. This seems always to have been an exit only.

Sources

BAL, RIBA Drawings, RAN 30 L/3[1].

Allan, J 1992. Berthold Lubetkin: *Architecture and the Tradition of Progress*, pp 243–4.

Coe, P and Reading, M 1981. *Lubetkin and Tecton: Architecture and Social Commitment*, p 146.

Pergola North of the Staff Car Park

The semicircular area across the Outer Circle from the Main Gate was laid out by Decimus Burton in 1830–1 as a carriage-sweep. From at least the mid 19th century there was an exit-only turnstile leading into the centre of this area. The semicircle came into use as the Zoo's car park around 1920 and the exit remained in use until much later.

A relic of the exit survives in the form of a two-bay iron pergola that adjoined the turnstile to the north. This comprises six slender (2 in./5 cm diameter) cast-iron columns, supporting L-section wrought-iron plates and T-section wrought-iron arches linked by multiple rods. The pergola now shelters a bench.

East Tunnel

Plan 4:26

The East Tunnel [**93** and **116**] is a pedestrian subway linking the Middle Gardens to the main part of the Zoo. Of the original entrance portals that to the south survives. It is classical in a manner that follows John Nash's Regent's Park work.

The tunnel is built of stuccoed brick with incised lines imitating ashlar inside the barrel vault (about 8 ft/2·5 m tall and wide). The south portal has a pedimented distyle-in-antis Doric screen above its roll-moulded and chamfered tunnel arch. A footway crosses in front of the screen on an outer arch with stucco voussoirs and a balustraded parapet between piers with reproduction urn finials. To either side the footway rises on curved wing walls with iron railings and end piers. The cutting to the south tunnel entrance is flanked by later retaining walls made up of brick and stone rubble salvaged from demolished Zoo buildings.

The hollow-quadrant moulded north tunnel arch lurks behind and under the faceted concrete of the Nuffield Building.

1829–30, Decimus Burton, architect; John and Samuel Dickson, builders; estimated cost £1,005. Listed Grade II.

93 The East Tunnel's classical south portal (BB92/28070).

94 The West Tunnel's north portal (BB92/6408).

West Tunnel

Plan 4:25

1919–20, in fulfilment of the 1913 scheme by Captain George Swinton with the Zoological Society of London's Garden Committee. Vault paintings 1954, by a team of students from the Royal Academy of Arts School of Painting working under Henry Rushbury.

The West Tunnel [94 and 95] is another pedestrian subway leading under the Outer Circle, made to improve circulation to and from the Middle Gardens in response to the increasing number of visitors. This was the first building work taken up after World War I.

The concrete tunnel vault is decorated with paintings in the style of those of the caves of Lascaux and Altamira. The cuttings to the tunnel entrances are flanked by high concrete walls with brick parapets returned across the tunnel entrances and articulated by piers with concrete urn finials and openwork panels of half-round tiles. Within the cuttings there are planted beds behind low stock-brick walls.

East Footbridge

Plan 4:11

1872, R Masefield and Company, founders; D Cross and Son, builders; cost £1,334. Abutments partly rebuilt 1930.

The East Footbridge [96 and 97] was erected to link the Middle Gardens to the Zoo's grounds north of the Regent's Canal, newly leased in 1869.

The bridge is of iron and bears the founder's name. There is circle-pattern ornamentation in the spandrels over the cast-iron arch ribs and in the iron balustrade panels on the 10 ft (3·1 m) wide deck. The substructure of lattice girders and crossed wrought-iron rods is identical to that of the 1864 Broad Walk (also known as the Cumberland or St Marks) Footbridge, located just outside the Zoo to the east (*see* Primrose Hill Footbridge below). The brick abutments have rendered dressings and balustraded parapets with urn finials.

95 *(Left) The West Tunnel interior from the north showing murals based on prehistoric cave paintings at Lascaux and Altamira (BB92/6406).*

96 *(Below left) The East Footbridge, built in 1872, from the south west (BB92/6411).*

97 *(Below) The East Footbridge, south spandrel and balustrade panels (east side) (BB92/6410).*

Primrose Hill Footbridge

1874 or 1879–80, to plans by John Fowler, engineer. Deck replaced 1906 and around 1930. Listed Grade II.

The Primrose Hill Footbridge [**98**] is a replacement of a suspension bridge of about 1842, one of five put up in Regent's Park by James Dredge, engineer, on a patent taper-chain principle. Another Dredge suspension bridge was replaced in 1864 by the Broad Walk Footbridge, located just east of the Zoo, following slippage of the canal bank. The latter bridge was made by Henry Grissell's Regent's Canal Ironworks, to plans by John Fowler, engineer. There was a gunpowder explosion on the canal in 1874 and further slippage of the banks occurred in 1879–80. The latter is more likely to have been the cause of the replacement of the Primrose Hill suspension bridge. The replacement bridge was identical to that surviving as the Broad Walk Footbridge.

98 The Primrose Hill Footbridge, showing south-east spandrel (BB92/6403).

96

In 1906 the Zoo expanded its premises north of the canal westwards up to the Primrose Hill Footbridge, the boundary of the gardens passing along the centre of the bridge. The deck was apparently then replaced to accommodate a divided footway. This wider deck (about 20 ft/6 m) was subsequently replaced by the existing narrower reinforced-concrete deck (13 ft/4 m wide) and railings.

Much of the late 19th-century bridge survives. There are I-beam segmental-arch ribs with ornamented spandrels. The substructure has lattice girders and crossed wrought-iron rods. The inner piers of the stone abutments were cut off at the level of the deck for the widening. The outer piers, with stiff-leaf ornamented cornices, were then reset on to concrete foundations.

Sources
Information kindly supplied by Malcolm Tucker.

99 The West Footbridge from the north west (BB92/6413).

West Footbridge

Plan 4:3

The West Footbridge [99] arose from Franz Stengelhofen's 1950 Development Plan. It was designed to improve links between the North and Middle Gardens and was ultimately built as part of the Cotton Terraces development.

The bridge forms an angular composition of pre-cast post-tensioned concrete. Its cantilevered side spans (56 ft/17 m long) rise slightly to a suspended central span (42 ft/12·7 m long).

1960–1, funded by Jack Cotton; Sir Hugh Casson, Neville Conder and Partners, architects (Frank Shaw, associate architect); Stephen Revesz, consulting engineer.

Most of the concrete has a coarse dark-blue shap aggregate finish, set off by smooth white Derby Spar aggregate on the balustrade panels and black finish on the insides of the balustrade piers. The wide deck is divided into two footways by four rectangular openings, two for staircases in the inner abutments and two for light-wells. These openings are enclosed by steel railings and teak handrails. At the centre of the deck, benches set on a plinth have replaced another lightwell. The banks under the bridge are paved with brick.

Sources
Architect and Building News, 19 Oct 1960, p 487.
Architect's Journal, 20 Oct 1960, p 566.
The Builder, 21 Oct 1960, pp 738–9.

7
Visitor
Amenities

Barclay Court (BB92/6303).

100 *The Parrot House, built in 1868–78 as the Zoo's Refreshment Rooms, from the south (BB91/28096).*

101 *The south-western porch of the Parrot House (formerly the Refreshment Rooms) showing the K3 reinforced-concrete telephone kiosk (BB92/6394).*

Parrot House (Refreshment Rooms)   Plan 4:56

The Parrot House [**100** to **104** and **111**] was built as the Zoo's Refreshment Rooms. (The building has been identified as the Fellows' Tea Pavilion of 1898. In fact this stood north of the Clock Tower.) It went up in three phases. The south block, or Dining Room, came first as a virtually free-standing adjunct to an iron-and-glass refreshment room of 1862 on the site of the north and west blocks. The replacement north block Refreshment Room was designed at the same time but the west block, built as a Second-Class Refreshment Room, was an afterthought, a fact that is evident in the meeting of the roofs. The north block later became the Fellows' Dining Room and the west block a Tea Room. Following the construction of the superior Regent Building Restaurant (*see* below), the whole building was converted for the display of parrots and diving birds.

1868–78 as the Refreshment Rooms; Anthony Salvin junior, architect; cost £6,636. (South block 1868–9. North block 1873; Simpson and Company, builders. West block 1877–8; George Smith and Company, builders.) Converted 1929–30 with addition of Garden Café and K3 telephone kiosk; Edward T Salter, architect. K3 telephone kiosk listed Grade II.

102 The former Dining Room of the Refreshment Rooms, now in the Parrot House (BB92/6395).

The building's picturesque *cottage orné* style is comparable to that of Salvin's 1869 Elephant and Rhinoceros House [**7**]. However, the asymmetry and apparent informality of the building are the accidental result of its accretive development rather than a stylistic device, each block being foursquare and symmetrical in itself. The walls are built of red brick, once again fashionable in the 1870s, with large mullion-and-transom windows under prominent gabled and half-hipped tiled roofs with ornamental bargeboards.

The south side of the south block has a central entrance with a stuccoed scroll-headed surround and formerly had a tiled tea terrace, now largely built over with brick lean-to and wire cage additions. The west side of the west block has ornamental entrance porches that formerly flanked a forward projecting outdoor serving counter under a glass roof.

Internally, the former Dining Room in the south block and the smaller former Refreshment Room/Fellows' Dining Room in the north block are similarly treated with cornices and elliptically vaulted ceilings. Cages have been inserted in the south block and the north block is now a linen store. The west block, the former

103 Plan of the Refreshment Rooms in 1929, prior to conversion to the Parrot House (based on Zoological Society of London Architects' Drawings – original in BAL, RIBA Drawings Collection, RAN 30 K/2). 1 Dining Room; 2 Fellows' Dining Room; 3 Tea Room; 4 Counter; 5 Wash-up Room; 6 Tea Terrace; 7 Porch

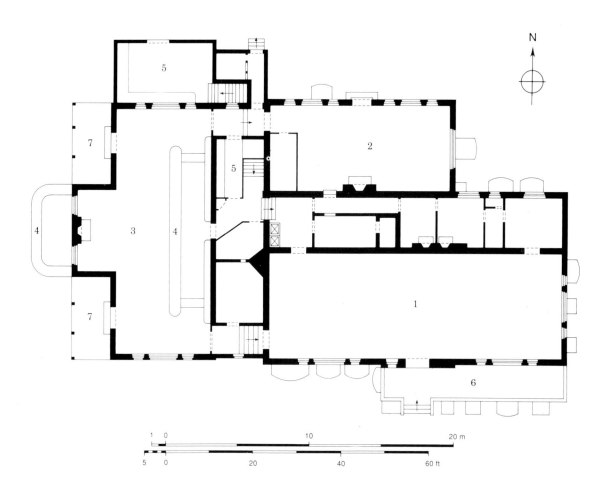

104 The basement kitchen of the former Refreshment Rooms (now the Parrot House) from the north east (BB92/6398).

Second-Class Refreshment Room, has a cornice to a coved ceiling. Service spaces form a T-plan between the three large rooms.

The basement had a large kitchen in the south block and a bakery in the north block. The former kitchen has two slender cast-iron columns supporting an I-section beam to what may be a fireproof ceiling. The western parts of the basement, formerly stores, are fireproofed with jack-arched ceilings of mass concrete on iron beams. Parts of the basement were latterly used as locust breeding rooms.

Attached to the north west is a large kiosk, formerly the Garden Café, a rebuilding of an earlier tea house. It is a low brown-brick block with gablets in a hipped roof.

A telephone kiosk under the south-western porch is a rare surviving example of the K3 type, designed by Sir Giles Gilbert Scott in 1928–9 as a reinforced-concrete variant of earlier boxes, but not successfully established.

Sources
BAL, RIBA Drawings, RAN 30 K/2[1].
Stamp, G 1989. *Telephone Boxes*, pp 11–12, 54.

Pavilion Building

Plan 4:51

The Pavilion Building [**105**] was put up as a tea pavilion. First set out as part of Captain George Swinton's 1913 redevelopment scheme, it was intended as the central of three buildings on the north side of a court looking down an axial walk. It is a development of the Italian Renaissance theme introduced by Joass in the Mappin Café.

Red-brick pilaster strips and brown-brick plinths articulate stuccoed elevations with steel-framed windows. The upper storey is reached only by external stairs on the return elevations. Heavily bracketed eaves disguise a flat roof with metal balustrade panels between urns, which originally stood on low brick piers.

1921–2, John James Joass, architect; J Jarvis and Sons Limited, builders. Converted 1989; John S Bonnington Partnership, architects.

105 The Pavilion Building, John James Joass, architect, from the south east (BB92/6357).

The ground floor, converted to a gift shop, was originally a tea room with a simple panelled ceiling and a raised outdoor terrace to the south. A semicircular colonnade with a bandstand of 1924–5 formerly enclosed the terrace. The shop conversion involved the insertion of fibreglass palm and baobab trees. The first-floor room, with the roof terrace, was designed for special parties; since the 1960s it has been the Zoo's staff canteen. Its basement is a store.

Sources
BAL, RIBA Drawings, RAN 30 J/6[1–7].
The Builder, 30 June 1922, p 980.

Discovery Centre

Plan 4:70

1923–4, Walter, Hearn and Chuter, architects. Converted 1988.

The Discovery Centre, formerly the Penguin Café, was built as a 'cheap' or 'popular' tea house. It has since been remodelled as an exhibition space and shop. It was originally open-fronted between oak posts, with brick end walls and a rear lean-to behind a serving counter. There are bracketed eaves to a hipped and gabled steel-trussed roof with a long north skylight. The six-bay front is now glazed and shuttered between the posts.

Regent Building

Plan 4:50

The Regent Building or Restaurant [**106**, **107** and **108**] replaced the earlier Refreshment Rooms (now the Parrot House – *see* above). It was built to provide improved lunch, tea and dining facilities for visitors and Fellows. To fulfil part of the 1913 scheme for a focal court, Joass prepared detailed plans for this building in 1914–15, somewhat more sparingly ornamented than his other, more Italianate, Zoo essays. The plans were subsequently revised slightly, the work being held in abeyance pending completion of more urgent projects.

This is a large block built in 2 in. red brick with stone dressings and gauged-brick voussoirs, the outer bays of the seven-bay south front projecting forward as pavilions. It is generously fenestrated, for the most part with steel-framed small-pane casement windows. Ground-floor arcading over French windows has been all but obliterated to the south and east by ill-fitting flat-roofed additions. A south-facing veranda on the first floor has been enclosed behind large sash windows. The upper storey has large ten-light windows to east and west. The rear elevation is untidy and poorly detailed, even though it overlooks the Outer Circle.

The ground floor was originally the public restaurant, with a still room and servery to the west, a buffet to the east and an outdoor

1928–9, John James Joass, architect; G Godson and Sons, builders. First-floor veranda enclosed 1937. Addition to south 1965, Franz Stengelhofen, architect. Addition to east 1971, John Toovey, architect. First floor altered 1975. Ground floor altered 1983–4 and 1989–90.

106 *(Above) The Regent Building (Restaurant) from the east (BB92/6265).*

107 The Regent Building's east staircase, with patterned balustrading and brass handrails (BB92/6268).

terrace to the south. The indoor space is now divided as the Regent Café, the Raffles Bar and the Raffles Restaurant. The first-floor Regency Banqueting Suite, originally the Fellows' Restaurant, has also been refitted.

There is a grand staircase in the east pavilion with latticed iron balustrading and brass handrails. A second stair, similar but smaller, is in the north-west corner of the building giving quick access to and from the Outer Circle. The kitchens are all on the north side of the building.

Land to the west of the building was laid out as a Fellows' Tea Terrace and Lawn, the latter serving as the site of the Chimps' Tea Party in the 1930s. A pergola covers the path to the terrace from a 'Member's Gate' on the Outer Circle.

108 The Regent Building's first-floor Regency Banqueting Suite (BB92/6271).

Sources
BAL, RIBA Drawings, RAN 30 J/7$^{1-3}$ and J/8$^{1-11}$.
Building News, 3 Nov 1915, pp 500–1.
The Architect, May 1975, p 28.

Former South Gate Kiosk

Plan 4:58

There is a small refreshment kiosk built to serve the South Gate, an entrance subsequently closed then cleared in 1985. The painted brick building echoes the adjoining and contemporary New Lion Terraces (*see* above) with buttress-like screen walls.

1976, John Toovey, architect.

Shelter south of the Bird House   Plan 4:72

*1928, as a memorial to
F H T Streatfield, FZS, who
left a legacy of £300.*

This shelter [109] is a neat little edifice of thin plum-coloured brick with distyle-in-antis piers articulated by tiled courses. Timber benches stand on a tiled floor under a panelled ceiling and a hipped tiled roof.

Shelter north of the Northern Aviary

This long shelter, built in 1962–4 for open-air seating, formed part of the Northern (Snowdon) Aviary development (*see* above). Benches facing south to the Aviary stand under four flat roofs linked by steel pergolas. The roofs are on timber posts in front of stock-brick screen walling, the inner side of which is used for display panels providing information about the birds.

*109 (Above) Shelter south of the
Bird House, viewed from the
north (BB91/28093).*

*110 (Right) The interior of the
Amphitheatre with its tent-like
superstructure (BB92/6350).*

Amphitheatre
Plan 4:45

The Amphitheatre [110] was made for presentations and events. The stage and terraced seating were laid out on a lawn that had earlier been the site of the Chimps' Tea Party. The tensile tent superstructure comprises steel masts and a 600 m² canopy, originally made of PTFE (Teflon)-coated glass-fibre fabric.

South of the amphitheatre there is an iron pergola dating to the late 19th/early 20th century.

Sources
Forster, B 1985. 'The engineered use of coated fabrics in long span roofs'. *The Arup Journal* (Autumn), pp 7–12.

1982–5, initial design by John Toovey, architect, and Anthony Hunt Associates, engineers. Superstructure donated by Bovis Coverspan Limited and designed by Ove Arup and Partners (Brian Forster). Re-erected 1990 after collapse in a storm.

Lifewatch Centre
Plan 4:46

The Lifewatch Centre is a single-storey flat-roofed building erected as the Zoo's shop at the south end of what was formerly a rose garden. It has been converted to serve as an information centre and first aid station. Colourful animal silhouettes have been applied to the north wall.

1962, extended 1968. Converted 1989–90.

Playground
Plan 4:46

The playground south of the Amphitheatre was noted at the time of its laying out for the safety and creativity of its (now outmoded) design, particularly the use of car-tyre swings slung from stressed arches.

Sources
Design, Oct 1971, pp 64–7.

1971, John Toovey, architect; equipment by SMP (Landscapes) Limited; maze panel designs by Banks and Miles.

Picnic Terrace

The picnic terrace, laid out in about 1965 to the north of the Children's Zoo, has crazy paving, tables enclosed by low brick walls and a timber kiosk.

First Aid Station and South Gate Lavatories
Plan 4:77

The First Aid Station and South Gate Lavatories are single-storey brick buildings. The First Aid Station was built as a shop (and used by Granada Television for *Zoo Time*) before conversion to its present use.

1967, Franz Stengelhofen, architect. Converted 1985–6.

Main Gate Women's Lavatory

1973–4, John Toovey, architect.

This facility is concealed under rising ground between the Main Gate and the African Aviary.

Barclay Court

Plan 4:49

1989–90, with a £500,000 benefaction from Frederick and David Barclay; Clouston and Partners, landscape architects.

Barclay Court [**111**] was laid out as an improvement of the area in front of the Zoo's restaurant and shop. It intentionally recalls Captain George Swinton's 1913 scheme for a court on this site.

The octagonal fountain at the centre of the Court has a ring of water in polished reconstituted limestone. On the south side of the brick-paved court there are two octagonal steel and timber refreshment kiosks with tented heads, a design that appears to be based on the Raven's Cage (*see* above). A similar kiosk stands near the south entrance to the West Tunnel [**95**].

111 *(Above) Barclay Court's octagonal fountain, looking south east to the Parrot House (BB92/6302).*

8

Auxiliary Buildings

The Zoological Society of London
Offices and Library
(BB92/6293).

Zoological Society of London Offices and Library   Plan 4:13

1909–10, John James Joass, architect; G Godson and Sons, builders; lift made by Archibald Smith, Major and Stevens; cost £17,787. Attic and turret balustrading removed 1932. Library conversion 1965, funded by Wolfson Foundation; Franz Stengelhofen and Colin Wears, architects.

The Zoological Society of London Offices and Library building [**112**, **113** and **114**] was erected to replace premises in Hanover Square. The Society's move to Regent's Park was prompted by the need for convenient access to the Zoo and for greater space for a growing library. The building's angular elevations are characteristic of Joass, though Alastair Service has called this an 'unsuccessful experiment' in the development of Joass's style, somewhat redeemed by good detailing.

The ground floor and dressings are in Portland stone, the first floor in panelled Luton brick. There are steel-framed Crittall's windows and the attic and its clock turret originally had iron balustrading comparable to the first-floor balconies. The floors are of steel and concrete. The central bays house entrance spaces in front of the library. The end ranges accommodate smaller rooms, mainly offices.

The principal interior space in the building was originally the Society's Meeting Room and Library, a double-height room of about 60 ft (18 m) by 40 ft (12 m). It has since been divided horizontally and refitted as a reading room over book stacks (the Society's Meeting Rooms had moved to the Nuffield Building). Originally the room had book-lined walls with pilasters (Ionic over Doric) and an iron-railed gallery. It retains a skylit segmentally vaulted ceiling under a steel-trussed roof.

112 The Zoological Society of London Offices and Library (BB92/6294).

113 The Library Reading Room from the south (BB92/6289).

The building is entered via a domically vaulted circular lobby of a Soanian character that houses a bust of Sir Stamford Raffles. The lobby gives on to a pilastered entrance hall across the front. To the south east is the ground-floor Council Room, which has a strikingly curvilinear T-shaped table and paintings of Sir Stamford Raffles (by James Lonsdale, 1818), Sir Peter Chalmers Mitchell (by

114 The Council Room (BB92/6290).

William Nicholson, 1935) and others. On the west side of the building, stairs rise around a well housing an original panelled lift. A first-floor centre-front reading room has been divided to form offices. The second floor originally had private apartments for the Society's Secretary.

Sources
BAL, RIBA Drawings, RAN 30 J/3$^{1-8}$.
Building News, 6 May 1910, p 636.
Architectural Review, April 1911, pp 217–23.

Prosectorium   Plan 4:74

Immediately east of the Bird House there is a small single-storey brick building. This was built in 1908 as a prosectorium (pathology and post-mortem laboratory) for the Zoo's sanatorium, which stood in the yard behind the Bird House from 1909 to 1956.

Animal Hospital and Pathology Laboratory   Plan 4:27

1955–6, Franz Stengelhofen, architect.

The Animal Hospital and Pathology Laboratory (occupied by the Institute of Zoology's Department of Veterinary Science) was built as a 'Sanatorium and Quarantine Station' to replace the sanatorium north east of the Bird House (*see* Prosectorium above). The siting is deliberately remote from the Zoo's animal houses.

This is a simple two-storey five-bay yellow brick block with a pitched roof and small windows. On the ground floor there are offices, an operating theatre, an X-ray room, a food preparation area and animal dens around the west and south sides leading to outdoor cages in a walled yard. The first floor has offices, laboratories and large cages.

Wellcome Building   Plan 4:28

1963, Franz Stengelhofen, architect.

The Wellcome Building is a research centre built as the Wellcome Institute of Comparative Physiology. This Institute was established for the study of reproductive physiology by Zoological Society of London staff and Ford Foundation Fellows, and is now part of the Institute of Zoology.

This is an architecturally undistinguished concrete and brick building of three storeys with upper-storey rear balconies overlooking Regent's Park. The ground and first floors house offices, workshops and research laboratories. The second floor accommodates animal cages.

115 The Nuffield Building (BB92/6299).

Nuffield Building   Plan 4:14

The Nuffield Building [**115**, **116** and **117**] was erected (to plans prepared in 1962) as the Nuffield Institute of Comparative Medicine, for the study of disease in animals, with the Zoological Society of London's Meeting Rooms adjoining. The greater part of the building comprises research laboratories for what has now become part of the Institute of Zoology.

This is a forceful piece of Brutalist architecture. The ground floor and basement walls are of roughly shuttered concrete, with the ground floor divided by the East Tunnel's northern approach, which it enfolds or oppresses, according to taste. The oversailing first floor has coarse aggregate facing on pre-cast panels with continuous windows on the long elevations. The east return has a tall stair window. An upper storey is set back almost out of sight from the ground.

The Zoological Society of London Meeting Rooms occupy the east part of the ground floor. They are entered through doors in a glass wall via a lobby which features a cantilevered staircase, a

1964–5, Llewelyn-Davies, Weeks and Musgrave (Michael Huckstepp), architects.

116 (Right) The Nuffield Building, the northern approach to the East Tunnel (BB92/6298).

117 (Below) The Nuffield Building, lobby to the Zoological Society of London Meeting Rooms (BB92/6296).

mobile by Kenneth Martin (1967) and a bronze head of Lord Zuckerman by Dame Elisabeth Frink (1985). There is a large meeting room which seats 200 and a small room for 50, separated by movable partitioning.

The rest of the building is reached via a ramp up to a west entrance. There is a small lecture room on the ground floor while the upper storeys contain laboratories off spine corridors.

118 (Below) The Education Department and Centre for Life Studies from the east (BB92/6422).

Education Department and Centre for Life Studies Plan 4:1

The Zoo's Education Department and Centre for Life Studies [**118** and **119**] is used for the education of school parties, teachers and others, including zoo staff. It is in the far north-western corner of the Zoo grounds, off the track of most visitors, and on a site that allows access outside zoo hours. It is discreetly situated and purposely unobtrusive, set amidst trees on the north bank of the Regent's Canal.

The dominant elevational surfaces are the split-pitched roof slopes; these and the walls are covered with dark asbestos cement slates. The ends of the main block, which houses the Education

1973–5, partly funded by the Wolfson Foundation; Sir Hugh Casson, Neville Conder and Partners (Anthony Reich), architects; W M Glendinning Limited, contractors.

119 The Education Department and Centre for Life Studies foyer with mural and brick staircase (BB92/6420).

Department, have square oriel windows over entrances which lead to a foyer with a mural and a central brick staircase. On the south side there are two 100-seat lecture theatres, extended on columns over a footpath on the canal bank. To the north there are two classrooms. A south-facing clerestory lights offices on the first floor.

The two-storey north-west wing, the Centre for Life Studies, was an afterthought. It was originally an Inner London Education Authority Teachers' Centre and has spaces for tuition, research and the accommodation of small animals.

Sources
Architectural Review, June 1976, pp 373–6.

9

Service and Staff Buildings

South Canal Bank Staff Flats (BB92/6352).

East Service Gate Buildings

Plan 4:52 and 53

*Lodge, 1863–4. Extended
about 1909 when service
gate was formed. Former
bakery, 1929. Converted
1961–2.*

The East Service Gate is to the north of the Pavilion Building. To its east there is a lodge [**Plan 4:53**] that was originally the Head Keeper's Quarters. Given its probable date of construction its architect may have been Anthony Salvin junior. Latterly it has been used as a storage area and as meeting rooms.

The building is a standard Victorian estate lodge of two storeys on a T-plan. It is built of red brick, largely painted white, and has slate roofs. There are garage additions on its north and south sides.

West of the service entrance stands a simple brick shed [**Plan 4:52**] which was built as a bakery for the nearby Regent and Pavilion Buildings, to replace the bakery in the basement of the Refreshment Rooms building (now the Parrot House). It was converted for use as a supplies building.

West Service Gate Buildings

Plan 4:29, 30 and 31

*1951 and 1958–60, Franz
Stengelhofen, architect.
(Services Building and
Garage, 1960. Works
Department, 1958–9. Boiler
House, 1951; Incinerator
added 1959, replaced 1982.)*

The buildings around the West Service Gate, to the north of the Mappin Terraces, derive from a 1950 plan for a new service complex that was incorporated into the 1958 redevelopment scheme prepared under Sir Hugh Casson. They were the first part of this scheme to be executed as the shifting of supply and works functions from the Middle Gardens to this site made space available for the Cotton Terraces. The buildings are discreetly situated behind the Mappin Terraces, but have good access for the movement of supplies and equipment.

The block east of the gate is known as the Services Building [**120** and **Plan 4:30**]. Built as a supplies store with some offices it is a two-storey, eighteen-bay flat-roofed range with a pre-cast concrete frame and cavity-brick wall panels. The lower storey has, from west to east, a general store, a hay store, a deep freeze for meat and an abattoir. The upper storey houses offices with, to the east, general and hay stores. There are louvred panels ventilating the hay store sections. To the east there is a garage with a monopitch space-frame roof. Built to house the Zoo's service vehicles, this replaced pony stables on the same site.

A space-frame canopy extends across the West Service Gate to link the Services Building to the Works Department block [**Plan 4:29**]. Comparable to the Services Building in construction, the latter comprises a two-storey, five-bay front block with ground-floor workshops and first-floor offices and a single-storey, seven-bay workshop block to the rear.

South of the Services Building and abutting the Mappin Terraces is the central Boiler House and Incinerator [**Plan 4:31**]. The yellow-brick boiler house was built to house two oil-fired boilers to replace thirty boilers distributed around the grounds.

120 The Services Building from the west (BB92/6367).

Gardening Department

Plan 4:9

The north bank of the Regent's Canal, east of the East Footbridge, has been the site of greenhouses since about 1920; standing buildings are of 1963 and later. The Zoo's Gardening Department propagates plants here, including many exotic species, for the enclosures and the public spaces of the gardens. The greenhouses have been rebuilt with a brick stores range to the north.

Keepers' Lodge

Plan 4:42

The Keepers' Lodge, built in 1903 [**121**], is a divided block of staff housing. The east section consists of a house designed for a head-keeper. The west section consists of lodgings (eight small bedrooms, a common room, bathroom and kitchen) intended for resident helpers. They combine to form an asymmetrical semi-detached house facing the Outer Circle. The upper storey is roughcast, over red brick, and there is ornamental guttering.

South Canal Bank Staff Flats

Plan 4:12

1962–3, Franz Stengelhofen and Sir Peter Shepheard, architects.

The South Canal Bank Staff Flats were built as part of the landscaping of the whole of the Zoo's south canal bank. They were needed because the contemporaneous development of the Cotton Terraces involved the demolition of a Superintendent's House.

The stock-brick building makes use of its sloping site with two upper-level flats for curators built over offices. The flats have concrete balconies to the north, with entrances and clerestory lighting to the south.

Zoo Sports and Social Club

Plan 4:10

1963, Franz Stengelhofen, architect.

The Sports and Social Club for Zoo staff is a two-storey, flat-roofed brick block accommodating a bar, billiard room and caretaker's flat. It is very plain to the north with an entrance from Prince Albert Road. To the south there is an outdoor terrace overlooking the Regent's Canal.

10

Statues, Memorials and Markers

*Boundary Markers for
St Pancras and St Marylebone
parishes (BB92/6330).*

122 *Statue entitled* Stealing the Cubs *(BB91/28065).*

Stealing the Cubs

1906, donated by J B Wolff;
Henri Teixeira de Mattos,
sculptor.

The statue entitled *Stealing the Cubs* [**122**] stands to the west of Three Island Pond. Carved from marble at larger than life size, it is a work of considerable dramatic tension which represents a man fighting a lioness over two lion cubs. In recent years the statue has been moved back from a more prominent position on a three-step plinth. This move and the omission of the title from its descriptive plaque perhaps reflect sensitivity to the offence that some would now take to the subject matter.

War Memorial   Plan 4:59

1919, John James Joass,
architect. Moved 1952.

A memorial to the employees of the Zoological Society of London killed on active service in World Wars I and II stands to the east of Three Island Pond, having been moved from a site near the Main Gate [**66**]. Its design is taken from a medieval French *Lanterne des*

Morts at La Souterraine, in the Creuse valley. It is a Portland-stone octagonal turret about 16 ft (5 m) tall and 3 ft (1 m) across on a three-step plinth. There are attached shafts at the angles and round-headed openings below a pyramidal cap.

Bear and Child Statue

At the centre of the circulation area at the east end of the Children's Zoo there is a small bronze statue of a child riding a bear [**123**]. It stands on a Portland stone pedestal and was probably moved to this site when the surrounding pens were rebuilt and given their present layout.

1928, donated in memory of Sigismund Goetze by his widow; E M A, sculptor. Moved about 1977.

123 Bear and Child statue in the Children's Zoo (BB92/6386).

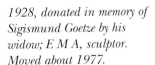

IN MEMORY
SIGISMUND GOETZE
PRESENTED BY HIS WIDOW

Bear Cub Statue (Winnie Memorial)

1981, donated by the Trustees of Pooh Properties; Lorne McKean, sculptor.

At the south-western corner of the Reptile House stands a bronze statue of a bear cub on a brick plinth [**124**]. Nearby there is a bronze dedication plaque. The statue commemorates Winnie, the American Black Bear from Winnipeg, who was resident on the Mappin Terraces from 1914 to 1934 and whose name was adopted by A A Milne for Winnie-the-Pooh. The statue was unveiled by Christopher Milne.

124 Bear Cub statue (The Winnie Memorial) from the south west (BB91/28069).

Guy the Gorilla Statue

1982, donated by William Timym, sculptor; cast by the Morris Singer Foundry.

On the south side of the Michael Sobell Pavilions for Apes and Monkeys is a bronze statue of Guy the Gorilla [**125**], a famous resident of the Zoo from 1947 to 1978. The larger-than-life bronze effigy stands on a plinth of reused granite kerbstones.

125 Guy the Gorilla statue (BB91/28064).

Globe Sundial

To the east of Three Island Pond there is a sundial in the form of an aluminium globe. The globe has an aluminium base with the cardinal points on a circular brick plinth. Triangular fins project from the globe over Roman numerals for the hours of the day; the fin casting the least shadow indicates the time.

1989, donated by Alcan Aluminium Limited; Wendy Taylor, sculptor.

Parish Boundary Markers

The boundary between the parishes of St Marylebone and St Pancras passes through the Zoo. Markers were put in place soon after the formation of Regent's Park and the Regent's Canal, and before the formation of the Zoological Gardens. Four pairs of these parish boundary markers survive within the Zoo: on the north bank of the canal just south of the Owl Aviary; on the south bank of the canal north of the Clore Pavilion; on the north side of the Outer Circle south east of the Clore Pavilion; and on the south side of the Outer Circle north of the Keepers' Lodge. Other pairs on the canal's north towpath and on the pavement on the south side of Prince Albert Road are just outside the Zoo.

There are heavily worn limestone posts for St Marylebone, of a 13 in. (33 cm) square section with chamfered corners. St Pancras has grooved cast-iron posts with 10 in. (24 cm) square bases tapering to octagonal heads. The posts carry parish initials and dates. They are of differing heights since ground levels have changed, but the stone posts appear to have been about 3 ft (1 m) tall, the iron posts about 2½ ft (80 cm).

1821, some replaced 1854.

127

List of General Sources

The most comprehensive account of the Zoo's buildings until now has been John Toovey's article '150 years of building at London Zoo' in S Zuckerman (ed) *The Zoological Society of London Symposium: 1826–1976 and Beyond* (1976), pp 179–202. This has a useful dated map and lists of architects and buildings in an appendix. Sir Peter Chalmers Mitchell's *Centenary History of the Zoological Society of London* (1929) is a good general history with particularly illuminating accounts of events during Mitchell's own time. The Zoological Society of London's Annual Reports generally include information on building work and the Zoo's Guide Books and their maps are often helpful. Additionally reference has been made to the Society's Architects' Drawings, held in the General Services Department at London Zoo. The Council Minutes of the Zoological Society of London and other primary sources in public archives were not consulted for the purposes of this survey.

A Series of ten Views of the Southern Portion of the Gardens of the Zoological Society in Regent's Park laid out to the Designs of D Burton, Esq., drawn on Stone by James Hakewill 1831.

Allan, J 1992. *Berthold Lubetkin: Architecture and the Tradition of Progress.*

Allibone, F and Karol, E 1989. 'Lions and tigers, no bears'. Notes for a joint Victorian and Thirties Society visit to Regent's Park Zoo, 19 March 1989.

Allibone, J 1987. *Anthony Salvin: Pioneer of Gothic Revival Architecture.*

Bartlett, A D 1900. *Wild Beasts in the 'Zoo'.*

Blunt, W 1976. *The Ark in the Park: The Zoo in the Nineteenth Century.*

British Architectural Library, Royal Institute of British Architects: Drawings Collection.

British Architectural Library, Royal Institute of British Architects: Biography Files.

Brook-Greaves, R B 1929. Drawn aerial view of London Zoo.

Burton, N: unpublished notes on early 19th-century central heating.

Cherry, B and Pevsner, N 1991. *London 3: North West* (*The Buildings of England* series).

City of Westminster, Marylebone Local Studies Library: photographs and cuttings.

Cline, R 1991. 'Regent's Park and Primrose Hill'. Unpublished dissertation.

Coe, P and Reading, M 1981. *Lubetkin and Tecton: Architecture and Social Commitment.*

Colvin, H M 1978. *A Biographical Dictionary of British Architects, 1660–1840.*

English Heritage (London Region): Historians' Files and photographs.

Gray, A S 1985. *Edwardian Architecture: A Biographical Dictionary.*

Greater London Record Office: photograph collection.

Hagenbeck, C 1909. *Beasts and Men.*

Hancocks, D 1971. *Animals and Architecture.*

Holloway, S 1976. *The London Zoo.*

Hulme, F W 1848. *Gardens of the Zoological Society.*

Huxley, J S 1939. *Official Guide to the Gardens and Aquarium of the Zoological Society of London.*

Institution of Civil Engineers Library: information on C B Trollope.

Miller, P 1981. *Decimus Burton, 1800–1881.* Exhibition catalogue, Building Centre Trust.

The Mirror, 6 Sept 1828, pp 148–9, and 29 Sept 1832, pp 280–1.

Mitchell, P C 1925. *Illustrated Official Guide to the London Zoological Society's Gardens in Regent's Park.*

Nairn, I 1966. *Nairn's London,* p 103.

Ordnance Survey maps: 1870 and later editions.

Post Office Directories

Public Record Office: WORK 32/65 and MPE/906, Decimus Burton's plans.

Scharf, G 1835. *Six Views of the Zoological Society's Gardens.*

Scherren, H 1905. *The Zoological Society of London.*

Sclater, P L 1876. *Guide to the Gardens of the Zoological Society of London.*

(ed) 1901. *A Record of the Progress of the Zoological Society of London during the Nineteenth Century.*

Service, A 1975. *Edwardian Architecture and its Origins.*

Thompson, G (ed) 1970. *The Encyclopaedia of London,* pp 594–5.

Vevers, G 1976. *London's Zoo.*

Victorian Society and Thirties Society 1992. *Creature Comforts: The Problems of London Zoo.*

Zenthon, E R 1960. Measured and drawn survey of London Zoo (National Monuments Record, RCHME).

Zoological Society of London 1951. *Zoo Blue Print: Looking into the Future.*

1976. *Golden Days: Historic Photographs of the London Zoo.*

Zuckerman, S (ed) 1976. *Zoological Society of London Symposium: 1826–1976 and Beyond.*

List of Recorded Buildings

The National Buildings Record (NBR), founded in 1941, is the principal national archive relating to historic buildings. It consists of photographs (currently numbering more than two million), measured drawings, reports, notes and other material and is constantly being updated. The NBR is housed at the headquarters of the Royal Commission on the Historical Monuments of England, Fortress House, 23 Savile Row, London W1X 2JQ, and the search room is open to the public during normal office hours. Copies of all Commission photographs can be purchased from the NBR. The following table shows the NBR File Numbers for the Royal Commission's London Zoo survey. These files contain supplementary material not published in this book.

National Buildings Record File Number: 90528
(London, Westminster, London Zoo, Regent's Park, NW1)

(All the buildings are in a Conservation Area)

NBR No.	National Grid Reference	Name	Type (Original/Present)	Grade, if listed
90528/1	TQ 2812 8346	Clock Tower	Animal House/Clock Tower	II
90528/2	TQ 2787 8349	Giraffe House	Giraffe House	II
90528/3	TQ 2828 8326	Bird House	Reptile House/Aviary	
90528/4	TQ 2804 8339	Stork and Ostrich House	Aviary	
90528/5	TQ 2813 8358	Insect House	Animal House	
90528/6	TQ 2801 8340	Reptile House	Reptile House	
90528/7	TQ 2809 8357	Gorilla House	Animal House	I
90528/8	TQ 2790 8352	Antelope Dens, Cotton Terraces	Animal House	
90528/9	TQ 2781 8348	Deer Dens, Cotton Terraces	Animal House	
90528/10	TQ 2791 8350	Camel and Llama House	Animal House	
90528/11	TQ 2782 8347	Horse and Cattle House	Animal House	
90528/12	TQ 2809 8335	Elephant and Rhino Pavilion	Elephant House	
90528/13	TQ 2803 8355	Charles Clore Pavilion for Mammals	Animal House	
90528/14	TQ 2805 8345	Michael Sobell Pavilions for Apes and Monkeys	Animal House	
90528/15	TQ 2822 8334	New Lion Terraces	Animal House	
90528/16	TQ 2819 8332	Water Birds Aviary	Aviary	
90528/17	TQ 2826 8332	Bollards east of New Lion Terraces	Bollards	
90528/18	TQ 2819 8335	Bollards west of New Lion Terraces	Bollards	
90528/19	TQ 2795 8340	Mappin Terraces	Panorama	II
90528/20	TQ 2796 8335	Mappin Café	Tea House	II
90528/21	TQ 2796 8342	Aquarium	Aquarium	II
90528/22	TQ 2811 8349	Raven's Cage	Aviary	II
90528/23	TQ 2808 8350	African Aviary	Aviary	
90528/24	TQ 2827 8330	Peafowl Aviary	Aviary	
90528/25	TQ 2800 8335	Southern Aviary	Aviary	
90528/26	TQ 2799 8362	Owls' Aviary	Aviary	

NBR No.	National Grid Reference	Name	Type (Original/Present)	Grade, if listed
90528/27	TQ 2794 8360	North Pheasantry	Aviary	
90528/28	TQ 2814 8366	Owls' Aviary	Aviary and Public Toilet	
90528/29	TQ 2825 8350	Parrot Aviary	Aviary and Public Toilet	
90528/30	TQ 2815 8341	Gibbon Cage	Aviary	
90528/31	TQ 2817 8344	Cockatoo Aviary	Aviary	
90528/32	TQ 2824 8324	South Pheasantry	Aviary	
90528/33	TQ 2789 8356	Northern Aviary	Aviary	
90528/34	TQ 2823 8338	Three Island Pond	Pond	
90528/35	TQ 2822 8341	Former Prairie Dog Enclosure	Pen	
90528/36	TQ 2803 8335	Sea Lion Pond	Sea Lion Pool	
90528/37	TQ 2803 8333	Sea Lion Pond Viewing Stand	Grandstand	
90528/38	TQ 2813 8357	Prairie Marmot Enclosure	Pond	
90528/39	TQ 2797 8353	Reptiliary	Pen	
90528/40	TQ 2813 8332	Mongoose Enclosure	Pen	
90528/41	TQ 2818 8330	Penguin Pool	Penguin Pool	I
90528/42	TQ 2814 8331	Cormorant Pond	Pond	
90528/43	TQ 2813 8329	Penguin Incubation Centre	Pond	
90528/44	TQ 2811 8329	Children's Zoo Deer Shed	Deer House	
90528/45	TQ 2814 8328	Children's Zoo Stables	Stable	
90528/46	TQ 2816 8327	Children's Zoo Nocturnal House	Animal House	
90528/47	TQ 2821 8325	Children's Zoo Milking Parlour	Milking Parlour	
90528/48	TQ 2819 8326	Children's Zoo Cow Shed	Cow Shed	
90528/49	TQ 2818 8326	Children's Zoo Shed	Shed/Offices	
90528/50	TQ 2818 8325	Children's Zoo Animal Handling Building	Animal House	
90528/51	TQ 2822 8324	Children's Zoo Farm Pens	Pen	
90528/52	TQ 2832 8328	Wolf Wood	Pen	
90528/53	TQ 2823 8350	Flamingo Pool	Pond	
90528/54	TQ 2811 8356	Otter Pool	Pond	
90528/55	TQ 2801 8348	Main Gate	Gate	
90528/56	TQ 2807 8365	North Gate	Gate and Public Toilet/Aviary	
90528/57	TQ 2810 8365	North Gate Kiosk	Refreshment Pavilion/Aviary	II
90528/58	TQ 2809 8365	North Gate Exit Turnstiles	Turnstile	
90528/59	TQ 2799 8352	Pergola North of Staff Car Park	Pergola	
90528/60	TQ 2817 8356	East Tunnel	Tunnel	II
90528/61	TQ 2797 8348	West Tunnel	Tunnel	
90528/62	TQ 2815 8363	East Footbridge	Footbridge	
90528/63	TQ 2777 8348	Primrose Hill Footbridge	Footbridge	II
90528/64	TQ 2793 8356	West Footbridge	Footbridge	
90528/65	TQ 2824 8346	Parrot House	Refreshment Rooms/Aviary	
90528/66	TQ 2822 8347	Former Garden Café	Café	
90528/67	TQ 2822 8346	K3 Type Telephone Kiosk	Telephone Box	II
90528/68	TQ 2820 8353	Pavilion Building	Tea House/Shop	
90528/69	TQ 2818 8327	Discovery Centre	Tea House/Shop	
90528/70	TQ 2815 8352	Regent Building	Restaurant	

Recorded Buildings

NBR No.	National Grid Reference	Name	Type (Original/Present)	Grade, if listed
90528/71	TQ 2826 8336	Former South Gate Kiosk	Refreshment Pavilion	
90528/72	TQ 2829 8323	Shelter south of Bird House	Garden Seat	
90528/73	TQ 2788 8358	Shelter north of Northern Aviary	Garden Seat	
90528/74	TQ 2815 8345	Amphitheatre	Theatre	
90528/75	TQ 2814 8344	Pergola south of Amphitheatre	Pergola	
90528/76	TQ 2812 8341	Lifewatch Centre	Shop	
90528/77	TQ 2813 8343	Playground	Playground	
90528/78	TQ 2815 8329	Picnic Terrace	Garden Terrace	
90528/79	TQ 2828 8332	First Aid Station	Shop	
90528/80	TQ 2828 8333	South Gate Lavatories	Public Toilet	
90528/81	TQ 2806 8348	Main Gate Women's Lavatory	Public Toilet	
90528/82	TQ 2818 8348	Barclay Court Fountain	Fountain	
90528/83	TQ 2816 8346	Kiosk south west of Barclay Court	Refreshment Pavilion	
90528/84	TQ 2820 8346	Kiosk south east of Barclay Court	Refreshment Pavilion	
90528/85	TQ 2798 8345	Kiosk south of West Tunnel	Refreshment Pavilion	
90528/86	TQ 2821 8360	Zoological Society of London Offices and Library	Administration Block	
90528/87	TQ 2780 8353	Education Department and Centre for Life Studies	School/Teachers' Centre	
90528/88	TQ 2817 8359	Nuffield Building	Laboratory	
90528/89	TQ 2785 8340	Wellcome Building	Laboratory	
90528/90	TQ 2783 8340	Animal Hospital and Pathology Laboratory	Hospital	
90528/91	TQ 2790 8343	Services Building	Storehouse	
90528/92	TQ 2796 8345	Garage	Garage	
90528/93	TQ 2787 8341	Works Department	Workshop	
90528/94	TQ 2791 8342	Boiler House and Incinerator	Boiler House and Incinerator	
90528/95	TQ 2823 8356	Lodge at East Service Gate	Lodge	
90528/96	TQ 2821 8355	Former Bakery at East Service Gate	Bakery/Storehouse	
90528/97	TQ 2817 8366	Gardening Department Greenhouses	Greenhouses	
90528/98	TQ 2810 8351	Keepers' Lodge	Lodging House	
90528/99	TQ 2820 8362	South Canal Bank Staff Flats	Flats	
90528/100	TQ 2820 8366	Zoological Society of London Sports and Social Club	Club	
90528/101	TQ 2821 8340	Stealing the Cubs	Statue	
90528/102	TQ 2825 8340	War Memorial	War Memorial	
90528/103	TQ 2821 8324	Bear and Child Statue	Statue'	
90528/104	TQ 2799 8338	Bear Cub Statue	Statue	
90528/105	TQ 2804 8342	Guy the Gorilla Statue	Statue	
90528/106	TQ 2825 8334	Lion's Head Sculpture	Sculpture	
90528/107	TQ 2827 8339	Globe Sundial	Sundial	
90528/108	TQ 2827 8345	Hand Sculpture	Sculpture	
90528/109	TQ 2785 8356	Bird Sculpture	Sculpture	
90528/110	TQ 2801 8361	Parish Boundary Markers	Boundary Markers	
90528/111	TQ 2804 8358	Parish Boundary Markers	Boundary Markers	
90528/112	TQ 2808 8353	Parish Boundary Markers	Boundary Markers	
90528/113	TQ 2810 8352	Parish Boundary Markers	Boundary Markers	

Index

(Page numbers in italics refer to illustrations)

Index

Plans of
London Zoo

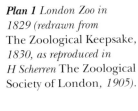

Plan 1 *London Zoo in* *1829 (redrawn from* The Zoological Keepsake, *1830, as reproduced in* H Scherren The Zoological Society of London, *1905).*

1 Entrance Lodges
2 Terrace
3 Bears' Pit
4 Rustic Seat
5 Llamas' House
6 Lawn and Pond
7 House and Cage for Macaws
8 Court Yard
9 Yard for Kangaroos, etc
10 Yard and Shed for Deer
11 Dens for Large Quadrupeds
12 Repository
13 Shed and Enclosures for Goats
14 Carpenters' Yard, etc

15 Dogs' and Foxes' Cages
16 Peccaries' Sties
17 Movable Aviaries
18 Monkey Poles
19 Otters' Cage and Pond
20 Monkey House
21 Beavers' Pond
22 Falcons' Aviary
23 Aviary for Small Birds
24 Pond for Small Ducks
25 Cow Shed and Yards
26 Owls' Cages
27 Turtle Doves' Cage
28 Enclosure for Rabbits
29 Eagles' Aviary
30 Guinea Pigs' Enclosure
31 Wolf's Den
32 Pond for Geese, etc
33 Large Aviaries
34 Keepers' Apartments
35 Enclosure for Pelicans
36 Emus' House and Yard

Key

Roofed houses and other buildings

Open cages and enclosures

Grass and shrubbery

Water

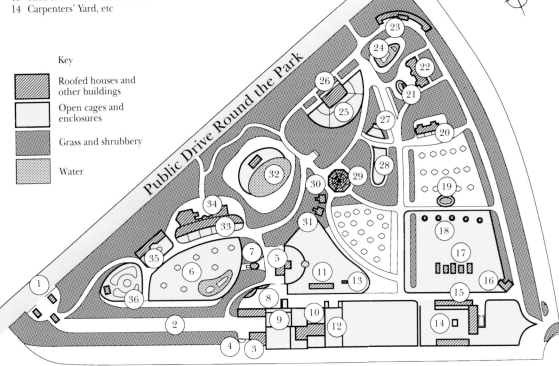

Public Drive Round the Park

10 0   50   100   150 m

50 0   250   500 ft

The Buildings of London Zoo

Plan 2 *London Zoo in 1893–4*
(based on Ordnance Survey
1:2 500 map).

1 Insect House
2 Northern Aviary
3 Zebra House
4 Giraffe House
5 Hippopotamus House
6 Superintendent's Office
7 Elephant and Rhinoceros
  House
8 Parrot House
9 Western Aviary
10 Monkey House
11 Camel House
12 Southern Ponds
13 Antelope House
14 Refreshment Rooms
15 Lion House
16 Reptile House
17 Carnivora Terrace
18 Lecture Room, Sloth, Ape
  and Small Cat Houses
  (including former Reptile
  House)
19 Three Island Pond
20 Great Aviary
21 Fish House

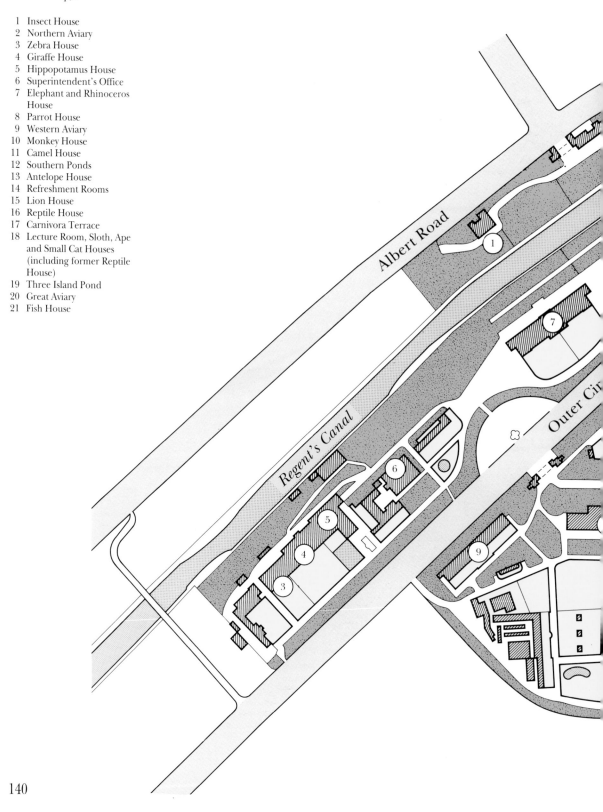

Plan 2

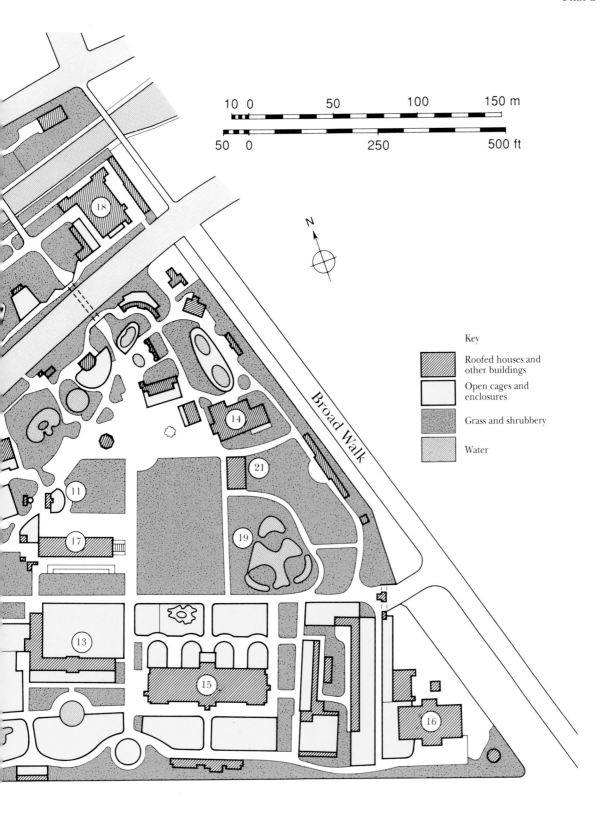

Key

Roofed houses and
other buildings

Open cages and
enclosures

Grass and shrubbery

Water

Broad Walk

141

The Buildings of London Zoo

Plan 3 *London Zoo in*
1929 (based on a plan in
P C Mitchell Centenary History
of the Zoological Society of
London *(1929) and a drawn*
aerial view of London Zoo (1929)
by R B Brook-Greaves).

1 Pheasantries
2 Giraffe House
3 Hippopotamus House
4 Curator's House
5 Elephant and Rhinoceros House
6 Caird Insect House
7 Small Mammal House
8 Offices and Library
9 Western Aviary
10 Main Gate and Entrance Court
11 Eastern Aviary
12 Restaurant
13 Tea-House and Bandstand
14 Mappin Terraces and
    Aquarium
15 Monkey House
16 Reptile House
17 Stork and Ostrich House
18 Antelope House
19 Lion House
20 Three Island Pond
21 Birds of Prey Aviaries
22 Deer and Cattle House
23 Bird House
24 Sanatorium
25 Park Paddocks
26 Monkey Hill

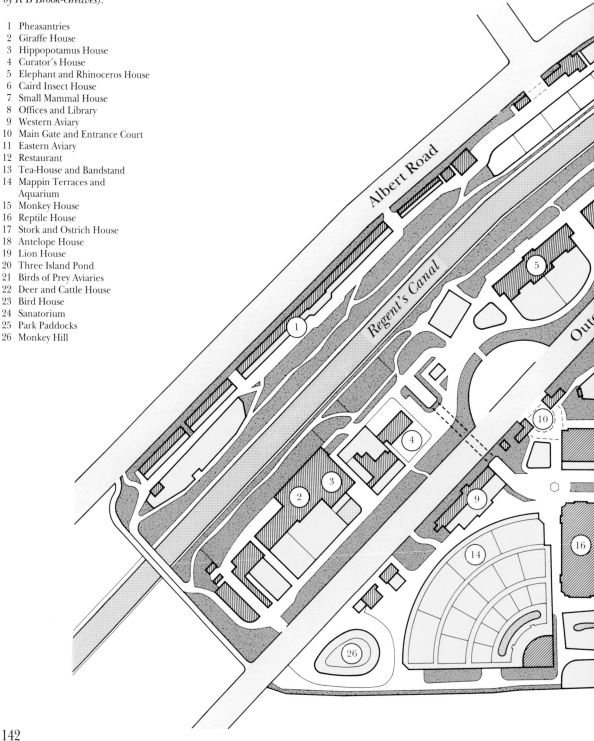

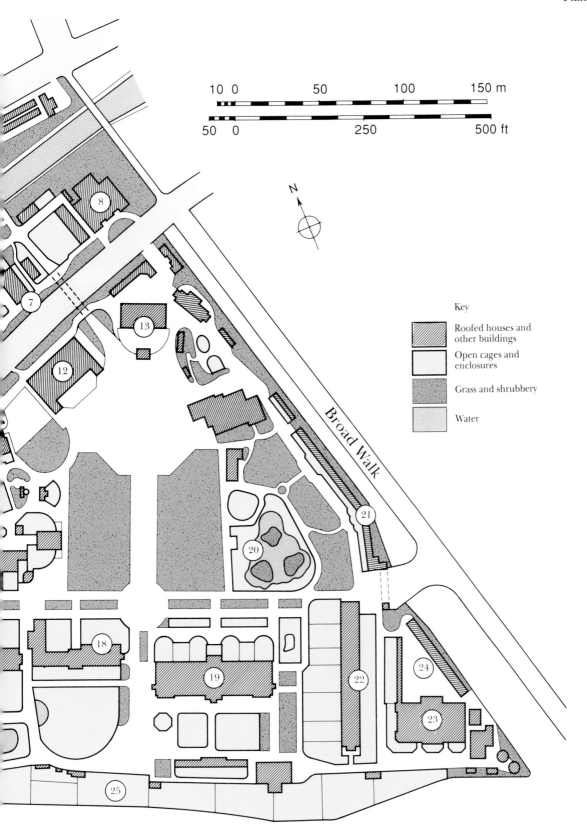

10 0   50   100   150 m

50 0   250   500 ft

N

Broad Walk

Key

Roofed houses and
other buildings

Open cages and
enclosures

Grass and shrubbery

Water

The Buildings of London Zoo

Plan 4 *London Zoo in 1991 (based on a plan by the Zoological Society of London Architects' Department, and RCHME site survey).*

1   Education Department and Centre for Life Studies
2   Northern (Snowdon) Aviary
3   West Footbridge
4   North Pheasantry
5   Owls' Aviary
6   North Gate (Bird Incubation and Rearing Centre)
7   North Gate Kiosk
8   Owls' Aviary and Public Toilet
9   Gardening Department
10 Zoo Sports and Social Club
11 East Footbridge
12 South Canal Bank Staff Flats
13 Zoological Society of London Offices and Library
14 Nuffield Building
15 Insect House
16 Otter Pool
17 Gorilla House (Koala House)
18 Charles Clore Pavilion for Mammals
19 Reptiliary
20 Camel and Llama House
21 Giraffe House
22 Horse and Cattle House
23 Deer and Antelope Enclosures, Cotton Terraces
24 Primrose Hill Footbridge
25 West Tunnel
26 East Tunnel
27 Animal Hospital and Pathology Laboratory
28 Wellcome Building
29 Works Department

30 Services Building and Garage
31 Boiler House and Incinerator
32 Main Gate
33 Mappin Terraces (with Aquarium)
34 Mappin Café
35 Southern Aviary
36 Reptile House
37 Stork and Ostrich House
38 Sea Lion Pond and Viewing Stand
39 Elephant and Rhino Pavilion
40 Michael Sobell Pavilions for Apes and Monkeys
41 African Aviary
42 Keepers' Lodge
43 Raven's Cage
44 Clock Tower
45 Amphitheatre
46 Playground and Lifewatch Centre
47 Gibbon Cage
48 Cockatoo Aviary
49 Barclay Court
50 Regent Building
51 Pavilion Building
52 Former Bakery, East Service Gate
53 East Service Gate Lodge

54 Flamingo Pool
55 Parrot Aviary and Public Toilet
56 Parrot House
57 Three Island Pond
58 Former South Gate Kiosk
59 War Memorial
60 New Lion Terraces
61 Water Birds' Aviary
62 Penguin Pool
63 Cormorant Pond
64 Mongoose Enclosure
65 Penguin Incubation Centre
66 Children's Zoo Stables
67 Children's Zoo Animal Handling Building
68 Children's Zoo Milking Parlour
69 Children's Zoo Farm Pens
70 Discovery Centre

71 South Pheasantry
72 Shelter
73 Bird House
74 Former Prosectorium
75 Wolf Wood
76 Peafowl Aviary
77 First Aid Station and South Gate Toilets

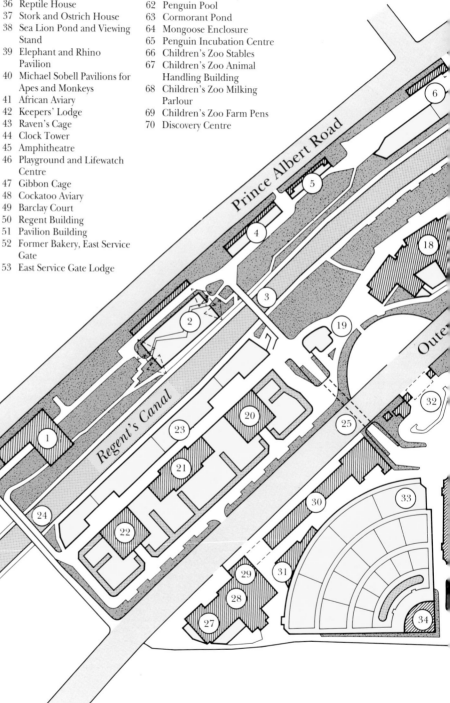

10 0   50   100   150 m

50 0   250   500 ft

N

Broad Walk

Key

Roofed houses and other buildings

Open cages and enclosures

Grass and shrubbery

Water